30 Minute Meals
for families

30 Minute Meals
for families

SHAUNA EVANS

FRONT TABLE BOOKS
An Imprint of Cedar Fort, Inc.
Springville, Utah

The opinions and views expressed herein belong solely to the author and do not necessarily represent the opinions or views of Cedar Fort, Inc. Permission for the use of sources, graphics, and photos is also solely the responsibility of the author.

ISBN 13: 978-1-4621-1428-3

Published by Front Table Books, an imprint of Cedar Fort, Inc.
2373 W. 700 S., Springville, UT 84663
Distributed by Cedar Fort, Inc., www.cedarfort.com

Library of Congress Cataloging-in-Publication Data on file

Cover and page design by Erica Dixon
Cover design © 2014 by Lyle Mortimer
Edited by Casey J. Winters

Printed in China

10 9 8 7 6 5 4 3 2 1

To my five fantastic, accomplished children—
Madison, Jeremiah, Elle, Hayley, and Luke—
for making *30-Minute Meals* necessary

Contents

01 Introduction

03 **One:** Breakfast

24 **Two:** Sandwiches

35 **Three:** Salads

50 **Four:** Soups

66 **Five:** Casseroles

77 **Six:** Pastas

92 **Seven:** Chicken

110 **Eight:** Beef

128 **Nine:** Fish

- -

141 Measurement Equivalents Charts

143 Index

148 Also by Shauna Evans

Introduction

We all live busy, hurried lives, taking kids to sports practice, taking them to music or dance lessons, and helping them with homework. Ironically, we have a full plate of activities but are challenged when it comes to filling our dinner plates with home-cooked, nourishing, and tasty food. That is where *30-Minute Meals for Families* comes into the mix. This book is designed to help families eat less fast food by making food fast. With easy-to-prepare recipes, family meals do not need to be a thing of the past. On these pages, you will be equipped with yummy dishes that help save you money and time and enhance your family's nutritional health.

Time-Saving Tips for Meals

The less time we spend making meals, the more time we have with our families. Here are some tips and tricks to making meals quick.

Leftovers

Not only does incorporating leftovers cut down on food preparation, but it also saves you money. Too often leftovers are thrown out or wasted. By taking stock of leftovers and utilizing them in next-day recipes, you are being resourceful. Some of the recipes in this book actually call for leftover items, such as Country Biscuits and Gravy (p. 18) as well as Chicken and Stuffing Bake (p. 68). And if a recipe calls for chicken, don't be afraid to substitute turkey if you have that in the refrigerator from the night before, or substitute canned tuna in Chicken Noodle Casserole (p. 70) if you forgot to buy chicken. Be creative with leftovers. If you prepare salsa for Cheese and Chicken Quesadillas (p. 106), you can use it in Chicken Taquitos (p. 96) the following day.

Rotisserie Chicken

I use rotisserie chicken ninety-nine percent of the time whenever a recipe calls for cooked chicken. Rotisserie chicken is a good choice because it is cooked, hot, and already infused with seasoning and juices. All you have to do is remove the meat from the bone. Typically, a rotisserie chicken yields three cups of shredded meat. Also, even though the preparing and cooking has been done for you, I have noted that a rotisserie chicken is about the same price as three pounds of boneless, skinless chicken breasts.

1

Cook Once and Eat Twice

Cooking once and eating twice dramatically frees up time. Why not double a soup recipe or make two casseroles? The little bit of extra time spent one day eliminates having to prepare or cook at all the next. This is a good idea if you know a certain day will be particularly taxing or busy. There is something quite comforting in the fact that a homemade meal is in the refrigerator or freezer waiting for you after a busy day of appointments, errands, work, and so on. This technique is also a fine way to save money. When your family is hungry and dinner is far from prepared, you are more apt to go out to eat, which invariably costs more and is likely less nutritious.

Freeze for Later Use

Preparing meals ahead of time and freezing for use on a later date is an excellent way to save loads of time. Many recipes in this cookbook freeze beautifully, including the soups, chili, casseroles, bakes, Bean and Beef Burrito Supreme (p. 120), and Chicken Taquitos (p. 96), to name a few. Wrap prepared dishes securely and label with the date and name.

Also remember that cooking times increase by about 15 minutes per frozen casserole to allow for thawing while baking. Do not thaw in advance; thawing will change the consistency in an unfavorable way. When reheating a prepared-ahead frozen meal, you will need to add ten to fifteen minutes to the baking time listed.

Keep Track of Inventory

One final and less obvious way to save time in the kitchen is to organize and keep track of the contents in your pantry, spice cabinet, refrigerator, and freezer. You may want to keep a running list, or simply keep everything tidy so you can take stock at a glance. By doing this, you will spend less time hunting down needed items for any given recipe. Also, you can plan meals based on what you already have on hand. This saves you trips to the grocery store and inadvertently saves your pocketbook. Studies have shown the more we shop, the more money we spend. To save money plus time, plan meals for a week and shop for needed ingredients once a week. A little preparation and thought in meal planning goes a long way in saving precious time.

BREAKFAST

04 Berry Banana
Morning Smoothie

07 Pan-Roasted
Potatoes and Ham

08 Eggs Benedict

10 Sausage and Egg
Mini Frittatas

12 Buttermilk Blueberry
Pancakes

13 Poached Eggs and Toast

15 Vegetable Cream Cheese
and Bagels

16 Ham and Egg
Breakfast Sandwiches

17 Bagel Breakfast
Egg Sandwiches

18 Country Biscuits
and Gravy

19 Bacon and Egg Omelet

20 Bananas Foster French
Toast

22 Apple and Walnut
Oatmeal

23 Peaches and Cream
Oatmeal

Berry Banana Morning Smoothie

SERVES 4

This all-fruit smoothie is a family favorite that includes our top three fruits. It is a vitamin C powerhouse as well as cool and refreshing. We love this for a quick breakfast.

1 cup frozen strawberries

1 cup frozen raspberries

2 oranges, squeezed

1 banana

- -

1. Combine all ingredients in a blender and puree.

2. Serve immediately.

Pan-Roasted Potatoes and Ham

SERVES 10

This hearty dish is perfect for breakfast. It is savory, with a lightly crispy skin, and soft on the inside. I could eat this as a main dish!

1 Tbsp. olive oil

1 Tbsp. butter

⅛ cup chopped red onion

⅛ cup chopped green pepper

1 tsp. crushed garlic

3 large baking potatoes, skins on, scrubbed and cut into 1-inch cubes

½ tsp. seasoned salt

½ tsp. sea salt

½ tsp. ground black pepper

1 Tbsp. dried parsley flakes

½ cup diced precooked ham

- -

1. Heat oil and butter in a large nonstick skillet over medium-high heat.

2. Add onion, green pepper, and garlic and sauté until soft, about 3 minutes.

3. In a bowl, toss potatoes with seasoned salt, sea salt, black pepper, and parsley flakes. Stir to coat potatoes.

4. Add potatoes and ham to skillet and turn heat to medium. Cover and cook for 5 minutes. Uncover potatoes and cook for an additional 15–20 minutes, or until potatoes are tender.

Eggs Benedict

SERVES 6

Personally, Eggs Benedict is one of my favorite breakfast dishes, especially for special occasions such as Father's or Mother's Day. Not only is it elegant, but it is also simple and delicious.

6 eggs

1 cup Hollandaise Sauce (see next page)

3 English muffins, split

6 tsp. butter

6 slices deli ham

⅛ cup fresh chervil, minced

- -

1. Poach the eggs: In a skillet with 2 inches of simmering water, carefully slide in cracked eggs. Let cook on medium-low heat until whites are no longer clear and yolk is starting to cook, about 8 minutes.

2. Meanwhile, prepare Hollandaise Sauce.

3. Toast English muffins and spread with 1 teaspoon of butter per half.

4. Top each half with 1 slice of ham followed by poached egg.

5. On each half, spoon 2 tablespoons Hollandaise Sauce over egg and sprinkle with 1 teaspoon fresh chervil.

Hollandaise Sauce -

Not only is this sauce delicious with Eggs Benedict, but it is also tasty on steamed asparagus or broccoli. Serves 10.

4 egg yolks

1 Tbsp. freshly squeezed lemon juice

½ cup butter, melted

⅛ cup fresh chervil, minced

¼ tsp. cayenne pepper

pinch of salt

1. In a stainless steel bowl, vigorously whisk the egg yolks and lemon juice together until the mixture has thickened and doubled in volume.

2. Place the bowl over a saucepan containing barely simmering water (or use a double boiler)—the water should not touch the bottom of the bowl.

3. Continue to whisk rapidly. Be careful not to let the eggs get too hot or they will scramble.

4. Slowly drizzle in the melted butter and continue to whisk until the sauce has thickened and doubled in volume.

5. Remove from heat and whisk in chervil, cayenne pepper, and salt. Cover and place in a warm spot until ready to use for Eggs Benedict. Note: If the sauce gets too thick, whisk in a few drops of warm water before serving.

Sausage and Egg Mini Frittatas

SERVES 12

These frittatas are like mini break-fast casseroles. This is a savory breakfast dish that is portable and nice to serve for dinner as well.

½ cup half-and-half

1 Tbsp. cornstarch

8 eggs, slightly beaten

½ tsp. black pepper

pinch of sugar

1 cup browned and crumbled sausage

1 roma tomato, seeded and diced

2 Tbsp. finely chopped green onion

2½ cups shredded mozzarella cheese

½ cup shredded parmesan cheese

fresh salsa for garnish

- -

1. Preheat oven to 350 degrees. In a large bowl, combine half-and-half and cornstarch. Stir until cornstarch is dissolved.

2. Add eggs, pepper, sugar, sausage, tomato, green onion, and cheeses.

3. Spray a 12-count muffin tin with cooking spray or fill with cupcake liners. Fill each cup ⅔ full with egg mixture.

4. Bake for 20 minutes or until toothpick comes out clean.

5. Serve warm with fresh salsa.

Buttermilk Blueberry Pancakes

SERVES 10

Homemade pancakes make breakfast special. Adding blueberries not only adds flavor and color but also packs a nutritional punch.

2 cups flour

¼ cup sugar

1½ tsp. baking powder

½ tsp. baking soda

¼ tsp. salt

2 cups buttermilk

2 large eggs

3 Tbsp. butter, melted

1 cup blueberries

butter for griddle and serving

toppings of choice

- -

1. In a large bowl, whisk together flour, sugar, baking powder, baking soda, and salt.

2. In a medium bowl, whisk together buttermilk and eggs. Pour the wet ingredients into the dry ingredients.

3. Stir gently until ingredients are almost incorporated. Batter will be lumpy.

4. Fold in cooled melted butter and blueberries. Heat skillet or griddle over medium heat.

5. On buttered griddle, pour ¼ cup batter for each pancake. Cook first side for 1–2 minutes. Turn when bubbles start to rise. Cook second side for about 1 minute or until golden brown. Serve with maple or fruit syrup or favorite toppings.

Poached Eggs and Toast

SERVES 4

Not only is this a simple and classic breakfast dish, but it is great for dinner as well. Since this recipe calls for ingredients most people have on hand, it can be made in a pinch.

1 Tbsp. white vinegar

4 large eggs

4 slices white bread

4 tsp. butter

½ tsp. dill weed

salt and pepper

- -

1. In medium skillet, pour in 2 inches of water, add vinegar, and heat to a simmer.

2. Crack eggs and slip into water.

3. Cook eggs for about 10 minutes.

4. Lift with slotted spoon.

5. Toast bread and spread 1 teaspoon butter over each slice.

6. Top each slice with poached egg and sprinkle with dill weed.

7. Add salt and pepper to taste.

Vegetable Cream Cheese and Bagels

SERVES 6

This is the perfect way to sneak vegetables into your child's breakfast. My children love the chewy texture of bagels slathered with a creamy topping like this one.

1 (8-oz.) pkg. cream cheese, softened

1 Tbsp. peeled and finely grated carrot

1 Tbsp. finely chopped green onion

1 Tbsp. finely chopped red pepper

6 bagels

- -

1. In a small bowl, combine cream cheese, carrot, onion, and red pepper.

2. Spread 1 tablespoon vegetable cream cheese over each bagel.

Ham and Egg Breakfast Sandwiches

SERVES 6

This is one of our family's favorite breakfast foods. The good news is they are easy and quick to make, and you can even take one with you as you begin your day.

butter

6 English muffins, split

6 eggs

6 slices Canadian bacon

6 slices American cheese

- -

1. Toast and butter English muffin halves.

2. In a large skillet, fry eggs in 1 tablespoon butter over medium heat, about 6 minutes, turning once. Remove the eggs and cover.

3. In the same skillet, heat Canadian bacon for about 1 minute, turning once.

4. On 6 English muffin halves, layer 1 egg, 1 slice of Canadian bacon, and 1 slice of cheese. Top with remaining muffin halves.

5. Serve immediately.

Bagel Breakfast Egg Sandwiches

SERVES 4

Adults and kids alike enjoy breakfast sandwiches. This is the perfect breakfast because it can be carried in one hand. Serve with simple fruit salad.

1 Tbsp. butter

4 eggs

4 bagels, sliced in half

8 slices prosciutto

4 slices mozzarella cheese

12 spinach leaves, washed and dried

- -

1. In a medium skillet, heat butter over medium heat.

2. Add eggs and cook to desired doneness, about 5 minutes, turning once.

3. Top 4 of the bagel halves with 1 fried egg, 2 slices of prosciutto, 1 slice of mozzarella, and 3 spinach leaves. Put remaining bagel halves on top.

Country Biscuits and Gravy

SERVES 12

This man-favorite recipe is comfort breakfast food, and it is simple and resourceful if you use leftover gravy from the night before.

2 cups flour

3 tsp. baking powder

½ cup butter

½ cup milk

1 tsp. salt

2 cups leftover gravy

- -

1. Preheat oven to 375 degrees.

2. In a medium bowl, sift flour and baking powder.

3. Using a pastry cutter, cut in butter until mixture resembles loose peas.

4. Add milk and salt and mix just until dry ingredients are moistened.

5. Scoop up golf ball–size chunks and form biscuits by hand.

6. Place on a greased cookie sheet and bake for 15–20 minutes, or until tops are golden brown.

7. Serve with ⅛ cup gravy over each biscuit.

Bacon and Egg Omelet

SERVES 1

For as long as I have remembered, I have loved omelets. They are easy and quick, yet sophisticated, and they are lovely for brunch and special occasions.

3 large eggs

2 Tbsp. milk

¼ tsp. pepper

1½ Tbsp. butter

3 strips bacon, cooked crispy and crumbled

¼ cup shredded swiss cheese

1 Tbsp. shredded parmesan cheese

- -

1. In a medium bowl, whisk eggs, milk, and pepper together.

2. Melt butter in a large skillet over medium heat.

3. Add egg mixture evenly in the pan and allow eggs to coat bottom of the pan.

4. Spread bacon and cheeses evenly over top of eggs. Cook for 1 minute.

5. Slide 1 side of omelet onto plate and fold one end over the top.

Bananas Foster French Toast

SERVES 6

Most of us think of bananas foster as a delightful dessert, but it makes a great topping for French toast as well.

3 eggs

⅓ cup 2% milk

1 Tbsp. fresh orange juice

½ tsp. cinnamon

1 Tbsp. butter

6 slices whole wheat bread

Topping:

3 Tbsp. butter

3 Tbsp. brown sugar

2 large bananas, sliced

real maple syrup

1. In a shallow bowl, combine eggs, milk, orange juice, and cinnamon.

2. In a large skillet or griddle, heat 1 tablespoon butter on medium heat.

3. Dip each slice of bread in French toast mix, coating each side, and place on the hot skillet.

4. Brown on each side, 6–7 minutes, turning once. Remove French toast to plate and cover to keep warm.

5. In the same skillet, heat 3 tablespoons butter until melted, and add brown sugar. Cook until sugar is dissolved.

6. Add bananas and cook until slightly golden brown. Spoon ¼ cup of banana topping over each French toast slice and top with syrup.

Apple and Walnut Oatmeal

SERVES 4

Oatmeal is a homey breakfast. When you add apples, walnuts, and cinnamon, it becomes not only more hardy and nutritious but also more delicious.

2 cups old-fashioned oats

3½ cups water

1 cup diced fuji apple (skin intact)

½ cup crushed walnuts

½ tsp. cinnamon

3 Tbsp. honey

milk

- -

1. In a medium pot over medium heat, add oatmeal, water, apple, walnuts, and cinnamon.

2. Stir occasionally until oatmeal is thick, about 2 minutes.

3. Remove from heat. Stir in honey.

4. Serve with milk.

Peaches and Cream Oatmeal

SERVES 6

You can make this comforting and flavorful breakfast ahead of time. Mornings are often rushed, so having breakfast prepared in advance is particularly nice.

3 cups quick-cook oats

1 cup peeled and sliced fresh peaches

⅓ cup brown sugar

2 tsp. baking powder

1 tsp. salt

1 tsp. ground cinnamon

2 eggs

1 cup milk, plus more for serving

½ cup butter, melted

- -

1. Preheat oven to 350 degrees.

2. In a large bowl, combine oats, peaches, brown sugar, baking powder, salt, and cinnamon.

3. In a medium bowl, whisk eggs, milk, and butter. Stir into oat mixture until well blended.

4. Spoon mixture into a greased 7 × 8 baking dish.

5. Bake for about 20 minutes, or until set.

6. Serve with milk.

SANDWICHES

25 Egg Salad Sandwiches

27 Turkey Club Wraps

28 Philly Cheesesteak Sandwiches

29 Reuben Sandwiches

30 Caprese Sandwiches

32 Marinara Meatball Sandwiches

33 Ham and Cheese Roll-Ups

34 Chicken Salad Croissants

Egg Salad Sandwiches

SERVES 6

Even as a young girl, I particularly liked egg salad sandwiches on soft white bread. It is a mild-flavored sandwich that suits picky palates.

6 large eggs, hard boiled

½ cup mayonnaise

1 tsp. dijon mustard

1 tsp. apple cider vinegar

¼ tsp. salt

¼ tsp. pepper

12 slices fresh white bread

- -

1. In a medium bowl, peel and chop eggs into medium chunks.

2. In a small bowl, combine mayonnaise, mustard, vinegar, salt, and pepper.

3. Add mayonnaise mixture to eggs. Fold to coat evenly.

4. Divide among 6 bread slices. Top with remaining bread slices.

Turkey Club Wraps

SERVES 4

Wraps make for scrumptious sandwiches. This recipe takes a classic club combo of turkey and bacon and turns it into a chic spinach-flavored wrap.

4 (8-inch) spinach flour tortillas

4 Tbsp. ranch dressing

12 slices deli smoked turkey

12 slices baby swiss cheese

8 bacon strips, cooked crispy

2 tomatoes, sliced thin

1 avocado, peeled, seed removed, and sliced into ¼-inch pieces

- -

1. On each spinach tortilla, spread 1 tablespoon of ranch dressing, leaving 1 inch around edges. Add 3 slices of turkey and cheese to each tortilla.

2. Evenly layer 2 bacon strips, 3 tomato slices, and avocado pieces over cheese.

3. Starting from one end, roll each tortilla up and then fold in each end.

4. Cut tortillas in half and serve immediately, or wrap in plastic and refrigerate.

Philly Cheesesteak Sandwiches

SERVES 6

You can't go to Philadelphia and not order a Philly cheesesteak sandwich. Fortunately, it's not necessary to go to our nation's first capital to experience this sandwich when you have this recipe.

1 Tbsp. olive oil

1 lb. flank steak, sliced into ⅛-inch-thick strips

1 cup thinly sliced green bell pepper

2 cloves garlic, minced

1 cup grated mozzarella cheese

6 hoagie buns, cut in half horizontally

- -

1. In a large skillet, cook olive oil and steak over medium heat, turning often, for about 6 minutes, or until steak is no longer pink.

2. Add pepper and garlic, and cook until tender, about 4 minutes.

3. Add cheese and melt, about 2 minutes.

4. Divide mixture among 6 hoagie bun halves. Top with remaining halves.

Reuben Sandwiches

SERVES 4

The Reuben sandwich is a favorite deli order, so why not make it at home for your family? This recipe combines tangy sauerkraut, savory pastrami, and creamy dressing to create sandwich perfection.

8 slices marbled rye and sourdough bread

1 lb. deli pastrami slices

8 slices swiss cheese

1 cup sauerkraut

2 Tbsp. Thousand Island Dressing (see below)

- -

1. On 4 slices of bread, divide pastrami, cheese, sauerkraut, and dressing.

2. Serve immediately.

Thousand Island Dressing -

Thousand Island Dressing is tasty on more than Reuben sandwiches. Go ahead and add it to hamburgers, salads, and other deli sandwiches. Makes 4 cups.

2 eggs, hard boiled

2 sweet pickles, chopped fine

1 (4-oz.) jar pimentos, drained

⅛ cup minced onion

2 cups mayonnaise

1 (12-oz.) bottle chili sauce

1. In a blender, puree eggs, pickles, pimentos, and onion. Add mayonnaise and chili sauce and puree. Refrigerate before serving.

Caprese Sandwiches

SERVES 4

You won't find a more simple and fresh sandwich than this. Caprese Sandwiches are especially good when tomatoes are in season.

1 French baguette, cut into 4 equal pieces

2 large tomatoes, sliced thin

½ lb. mozzarella slices

8 fresh basil leaves

2 Tbsp. olive oil

½ tsp. salt

½ tsp. pepper

1. Cut each baguette piece in half horizontally.

2. Divide tomatoes, mozzarella, and basil leaves among 4 baguette halves.

3. Sprinkle with olive oil, salt, and pepper.

4. Add remaining baguette halves on top and serve immediately.

Marinara Meatball Sandwiches

SERVES 4

This sandwich is hardy, filling, and my go-to recipe when I am in a time crunch. With the tomato-based marinara and meatballs, this is an Italian dish on a bun. And it's easy to transport and eat on the run.

20 precooked frozen meatballs

2 cups premium bottled marinara

4 (6-inch) hoagie buns, sliced horizontally

8 slices white American cheese

½ cup thinly sliced green bell pepper

½ cup sliced black olives

¼ cup finely grated parmesan cheese

1. In a medium stockpot, combine meatballs and marinara. Cook on medium-low heat until meatballs are completely heated through, about 20 minutes.

2. Over each of 4 hoagie halves, arrange 5 meatballs with marinara, 2 American cheese slices, 2 tablespoons bell pepper, 2 tablespoons olives, and 1 tablespoon parmesan cheese.

3. Top with remaining hoagie halves and serve.

Ham and Cheese Roll-Ups

SERVES 6

Even picky kids love ham and cheese. This is a tasty way to make a ham and cheese "sandwich" that kids love.

6 Tbsp. Honey Mustard (see below)

6 pieces flatbread

12 slices deli brown sugar ham

12 slices baby swiss cheese

12 slices red leaf lettuce

12 tomato slices

- -

1. Spread 1 tablespoon Honey Mustard evenly over each flatbread piece, followed by 2 slices of ham, cheese, lettuce, and tomato.

2. Starting from one end, roll up each flat bread piece.

3. Serve immediately.

Honey Mustard -

Not only is Honey Mustard delicious on deli sandwiches, but it is also a wonderful dip for chicken nuggets or popcorn chicken. Makes ½ cup.

⅓ cup mayonnaise

1 Tbsp. dijon mustard

1 Tbsp. honey

1. In a small bowl, whisk all ingredients until smooth. Chill before serving.

Chicken Salad Croissants

SERVES 4

This sweet-and-savory chicken salad sandwich combines chicken, fruit, and a creamy dressing, all on a buttery croissant. It makes a lovely luncheon dish. Why not add this gourmet sandwich to your child's or husband's lunchbox?

4 fuji apples

2 cups chicken cooked and cut into 1-inch cubes

½ cup chopped celery

½ cup dried cranberries

½ cup chopped green onions

½ cup pineapple tidbits

½ cup salted cashews

4 croissants, split in half

- -

Dressing:

1 cup coleslaw dressing

1 cup mayonnaise

- -

1. Core and cut apples, skin intact, into 1-inch chunks.

2. In a large bowl, combine apples, chicken, celery, cranberries, onions, pineapple tidbits, and cashews.

3. In a small bowl, combine coleslaw dressing and mayonnaise. Pour over chicken mixture and stir to combine.

4. Before serving, scoop 1 cup chicken salad mixture onto a croissant half and top with other half. Repeat for all croissants.

SALADS

36 Caesar Tortellini Salad

37 Italian Garden Salad

38 Prosciutto Salad Kebabs

39 Tortellini Salad

41 Caesar Chicken Salad

42 Chicken and Peanut Coleslaw Salad

44 Walking Taco Salad

45 Taco Salad

47 Green Chili and Beef Taco Salad

48 Mom's Tuna and Pasta Shell Salad

Caesar Tortellini Salad

SERVES 12

When I was in college, tortellini salad was often on the menu. It feeds a crowd, is inexpensive to make, and tastes great.

24 oz. cheese tortellini

2 cups shredded cooked chicken

1 cup un-marinated artichoke hearts, quartered

1 cup spinach, washed, dried, and torn into 2-inch pieces

½ cup feta cheese

½ cup chopped sun-dried tomatoes

1 cup prepared Caesar salad dressing

- -

1. In a large stockpot, cook tortellini according to package directions. (Note: tortellinis are done when they float.)

2. Drain tortellini and transfer to a large bowl. Toss all ingredients together except for Caesar dressing.

3. Just before serving, toss salad with dressing.

Italian Garden Salad

SERVES 10

This simple salad is especially good with pasta and Italian dishes.

1 head iceberg lettuce

1 small red onion, sliced

6 slices hard salami, cut into ½-inch strips

home-style croutons

2 cups spring greens

black olives

½ cup fresh grated parmesan cheese

3 ripe tomatoes, cut into eighths

Italian dressing

- -

1. Toss all ingredients in a large bowl except for dressing.

2. When ready to serve, toss with dressing.

Prosciutto Salad Kebabs

SERVES 8

It seems kebabs are the craze lately. If you can skewer it, you are right with the trend. Who would have thought a salad could be served on a stick? Here is a simple little prosciutto, mozzarella, and tomato salad just like that.

2 heads iceberg lettuce

8 (10-inch) wooden skewers

16 slices prosciutto

1 pint cherry tomatoes

1 lb. mini mozzarella balls

1 cup Ranch Dressing (see below)

- -

1. Cut each lettuce head into 8 wedges.

2. Twice on each skewer, thread 1 lettuce wedge, 1 prosciutto slice folded in half and rolled up, 2 cherry tomatoes, and 2 mozzarella balls.

3. Serve with Ranch Dressing.

Ranch Dressing -

½ cup buttermilk

⅓ cup mayonnaise

1 tsp. dried parsley

½ tsp. garlic powder

½ tsp. dried dill

½ tsp. salt

¼ tsp. black pepper

dash of Tabasco sauce

1. In a small bowl, combine all ingredients.

Tortellini Salad

SERVES 16

This is an excellent and quick potluck dish that kids and adults like equally. This salad offers lots of textures, vegetables, and tangy flavor.

1 (5-lb.) bag frozen cheese tortellini, cooked according to package directions

1 cup cherry tomatoes

1 cup fresh spinach broken into bite-size pieces

1 bunch green onion, chopped

½ cup hard salami slices cut into ½-inch strips

½ red pepper, seeded and chopped

½ cucumber, peeled and chopped into chunks

¼ cup crumbled feta cheese

⅛–¼ cup quality creamy Italian dressing

- -

1. In a large bowl, combine all ingredients and toss.

Caesar Chicken Salad

SERVES 8

One of the most popular salads is the Caesar salad. It is simple, calls for few ingredients, and tastes good with many different main dishes.

1 head romaine lettuce, washed and broken into bite-size pieces

1 pint cherry tomatoes

½ cup fresh grated parmesan cheese

2 cups shredded cooked chicken

1 cup croutons

1 cup Creamy Caesar Dressing (see below)

- -

1. In a large bowl, combine all ingredients except croutons and dressing.

2. Just before serving, toss with croutons and dressing.

Creamy Caesar Dressing -

Every home cook should have a homemade Caesar dressing recipe. This is a savory classic. Serves 10.

¾ cup mayonnaise

¼ cup olive oil

1 Tbsp. fresh lemon juice

4 cloves garlic, minced

1 tsp. worcestershire sauce

1 tsp. dijon mustard

¼ tsp. salt

¼ tsp. black pepper

1. In blender, combine all ingredients. Blend until smooth and all ingredients are incorporated.

Chicken and Peanut Coleslaw Salad

SERVES 16

Families love this is sweet-and-savory salad. It feeds a crowd. The chicken and peanuts add sufficient protein and extra flavor, making it a tasty dish well fitted for luncheons or potluck dinners.

1 bunch romaine lettuce

2 cups prepared coleslaw mix

1 cup fresh spinach, washed and dried

2 cups shredded cooked chicken

1 cup salted peanuts

1 cup dried cranberries

1 cup creamy poppy seed dressing
  (I use Brianna's poppy seed dressing)

- -

1. In a large bowl, combine all ingredients except dressing.

2. Just before serving, toss with dressing.

3. Serve immediately.

Walking Taco Salad

SERVES 6

What could be more fun or more convenient for busy families than Walking Taco Salad? My friend Tina introduced me to the concept in 2012. I thought the idea of putting salad in single-serving chip bags was clever and creative.

1 lb. hamburger

½ (1-oz.) pkg. taco seasoning mix, or homemade (p. 127)

1 (8-oz.) can tomato sauce

1 (15-oz.) can pinto beans, rinsed and drained

2 tomatoes, chopped fine

½ cup sliced olives

½ cup finely chopped green onions

2 cups mild cheddar cheese

4 cups romaine lettuce, torn into bite-size pieces

6 (2-oz.) individual-size bags nacho chips

salsa, sour cream, or ranch dressing

1. In a medium skillet, brown hamburger.

2. Add taco seasoning, tomato sauce, and beans. Cook on medium-low heat until heated through, about 5 minutes.

3. Divide meat mixture, tomatoes, olives, green onions, cheese, and lettuce among 6 open bags of nacho chips.

4. Garnish with salsa, sour cream, or ranch dressing.

Taco Salad

SERVES 6

Taco shell bowls create an authentic and restaurant-style twist to this easy, healthy, and delicious homemade recipe. Add fried ice cream or churros and this meal will feel like a fiesta.

1 lb. lean ground beef

1 cup picante salsa

1 Tbsp. chili powder

1 tsp. cumin

½ tsp. garlic powder

¼ tsp. salt

¼ tsp. black pepper

1 (14-oz.) can black beans, rinsed and drained

1 head romaine lettuce, washed and cut into medium pieces

3 tomatoes, diced

3 green onions, sliced thin

½ cup sour cream

½ cup guacamole

½ cup sliced black olives

6 taco shell bowls

- -

1. In a skillet over medium heat, brown hamburger.

2. Add salsa, chili powder, cumin, garlic powder, salt, and pepper. Stir to combine.

3. Simmer meat mixture for 10 minutes.

4. To assemble taco salad, divide meat, beans, lettuce, tomatoes, green onions, sour cream, guacamole, and black olives among taco shell bowls.

Green Chili and Beef Taco Salad

SERVES 12

In high school, I requested this taco salad weekly, so my mother changed the title on her recipe card to "Shauna's Favorite Taco Salad."

½ onion, diced

½ tsp. garlic powder

1 Tbsp. canola oil

1½ lbs. lean ground beef

1 (14-oz.) can cream of mushroom soup

1 (14-oz.) can enchilada sauce

1 (6-oz.) can diced green chilies

4 cups cheese-flavored tortilla chips

2 cups shredded colby and monterey jack cheese

2 cups shredded romaine lettuce

1 cup diced tomatoes

sour cream

½ cup diced green onions

½ cup sliced black olives

- -

1. In a skillet, sauté onion and garlic in oil until tender.

2. In the skillet with onion, add ground beef and cook until browned.

3. Add soup, enchilada sauce, and chilies to meat mixture.

4. Cook mixture on medium-low heat for 5 minutes or until heated through.

5. Layer bottom of a large casserole dish with tortilla chips followed by meat mixture, cheese, lettuce, tomatoes, sour cream, green onions, and olives.

Mom's Tuna and Pasta Shell Salad

SERVES 16

My mother created this recipe. It is mild but surprisingly satisfying with the pasta, tuna, and eggs. Mom's Tuna and Pasta Shell Salad is good alone or paired with fruit or barbecued or fried chicken.

4 cups small shell pasta, cooked (about 8 ounces dried)

2 (5-oz.) cans albacore tuna packed in water, drained

3 eggs, hard boiled and chopped into small chunks

½ cup sliced black olives

½ cup diced dill pickles

⅔ cup mayonnaise

2 Tbsp. dried onions

½ tsp. garlic powder

¼ tsp. black pepper

- -

1. Cook pasta according to directions on package. Drain well.

2. Add tuna, eggs, olives, and pickles. Toss to combine.

3. In a small bowl, combine mayonnaise, dried onions, garlic powder, and pepper.

4. Fold mayonnaise mixture into pasta salad. Stir to coat evenly.

SOUPS

51 Cheesy Potato Soup

52 Classic Chicken Noodle Soup

53 Quick Taco Soup

54 Chicken Taco Soup

56 Bahama Chicken Soup

58 Hungarian Beef and Potato Soup

59 Chicken and Rice Soup

60 Two-Bean Chili

62 South-of-the-Border Soup

63 Cheeseburger Soup

65 Chinese Chicken Noodle Soup

Cheesy Potato Soup

SERVES 10

Cheesy Potato Soup is savory and satisfying. For a touch of fun, serve in a bread bowl.

1 cup peeled and shredded carrots

½ cup chopped celery

1 small onion, chopped

¼ cup chopped fresh parsley, or 1 Tbsp. dried

6 Tbsp. butter, divided

2 Tbsp. oil

1 tsp. dried basil

¾ tsp. salt

½ tsp. pepper

4 cups potatoes peeled and cut into chunks

3 cups chicken broth

¼ cup flour

1½ cups milk

8 oz. mild cheddar cheese, shredded

¼ cup sour cream

1. Sauté carrots, celery, onion, and parsley in 2 tablespoons butter and 2 tablespoons olive oil for 5–10 minutes. Add basil, salt, and pepper. Transfer to stockpot. Add potatoes and chicken broth. Cook until potatoes are tender, 10–15 minutes.

2. **Make roux:** Melt 4 tablespoons butter in saucepan. Add flour. Mix. Add milk all at once and stir until thick and bubbly. Add to potato mixture. Stir.

3. Add cheese. Stir until melted and blended.

4. Add sour cream and stir. Serve in bread bowls.

Classic Chicken Noodle Soup

SERVES 12

Growing up in a climate where it is cool eight months out of the year, I gravitate toward soups and make a lot of them. Classic Chicken Noodle Soup is a mainstay on chilly days at our house.

2 Tbsp. olive oil

1 medium onion, chopped

4 stalks celery, chopped

3 cloves garlic, minced

6 cups water

3 cups chicken broth

1 chicken bouillon cube

1 (13-oz.) can cream of chicken soup

1 cup carrots peeled and cut into small chunks

3 cups shredded cooked chicken

½ Tbsp. dried oregano leaves

½ Tbsp. dried basil leaves

1 bay leaf

½ tsp. salt

½ tsp. black pepper

8 oz. egg noodles

1. In large stockpot, heat oil over medium heat. Add onion, celery, and garlic. Cook until vegetables are soft, about 4 minutes.

2. Add water, chicken broth, bouillon cube, cream of chicken soup, carrots, chicken, and seasonings. Cook on medium-low heat until carrots are tender, about 15 minutes.

3. Add egg noodles and cook until tender, about 9 minutes.

Quick Taco Soup

SERVES 12

With five active, accomplished children involved in dance, sports, music, and drama, I understand the need to get a satisfying and nourishing meal made fast. Quick Taco Soup helps me do just that.

1 Tbsp. olive oil

½ cup chopped onion

1 (14-oz.) can chicken broth

1 (10-oz.) can stewed tomatoes with green chilies, undrained

1 (15-oz.) can black beans, rinsed and drained

1 (15-oz.) can corn, undrained

1 (1.75-oz.) pkg. taco seasoning

2 cups shredded cooked chicken

tortilla chips

sour cream

shredded cheese

- -

1. In large stockpot over medium heat, cook oil and onion until tender, about 3 minutes.

2. Add broth, tomatoes, beans, corn, seasoning, and chicken.

3. Turn heat to low and simmer until heated through, 5–8 minutes.

4. Serve with tortilla chips, sour cream, and shredded cheese.

Chicken Taco Soup

SERVES 14

I grew up in a family of four boys and a football coach for a father, so game day was every Friday and Saturday in the fall months. As a result, we often made taco soup on game days. Here is a nice and hardy chicken taco soup recipe we love, especially during gridiron season.

1 Tbsp. olive oil

¾ cup chopped onion

2 cloves garlic, minced

2 cups shredded cooked chicken

2 (15-oz.) cans chicken broth

1 cup salsa

1 cup frozen corn

1 (10-oz.) can cilantro and lime stewed tomatoes

1 Tbsp. fresh lime juice

2 tsp. chili powder

1 tsp. ground cumin

1 (15-oz.) can black beans, rinsed and drained

Tortilla Strips (see next page)

colby and monterey jack cheese, shredded

sour cream

1. In large stockpot, heat oil over medium heat. Add onion and garlic. Cook until tender, about 4 minutes.

2. Add shredded chicken, broth, salsa, corn, tomatoes, lime juice, chili powder, and cumin. Cook 8 minutes.

3. Add beans and turn to low. Simmer for another 4 minutes.

4. Garnish with Tortilla Strips, cheese, and sour cream.

Tortilla Strips

Homemade tortilla strips are a snap to make and a tasty accompaniment to tortilla, taco, or Bahama soup. Serves 12.

4 Tbsp. butter

½ tsp. garlic powder

½ tsp. salt

6 (8-inch) flour tortillas

1. Preheat oven to 400 degrees.

2. Combine butter, garlic powder, and salt in microwave-safe bowl. On medium heat, cook in microwave for 25 seconds or until butter is melted.

3. Brush mixture on both sides of each flour tortilla.

4. Using a pizza cutter, cut tortillas in ½-inch strips.

5. Spread strips evenly on cookie sheet.

6. Bake for 8 minutes, turning once.

Bahama Chicken Soup

SERVES 12

This is a delightful recipe that I tried to re-create at home after dining at the Bahama Mama restaurant in Orlando, Florida. It has Thai flavors and influence with the coconut milk, lime, and cilantro. It is one of our family favorites.

1 Tbsp. canola oil

¾ cup diced onions

½ cup diced red bell pepper

2 cloves garlic, minced

1 Tbsp. seeded and minced jalapeño pepper

3 (15-oz.) cans chicken broth

2 (15-oz.) cans unsweetened coconut milk

1 (10-oz.) can cilantro and lime diced tomatoes, undrained

3 cups shredded cooked chicken

¾ cup diced carrots

½ cup cilantro, chopped

1 tsp. brown sugar

½ tsp. salt

½ tsp. pepper

Tortilla Strips (p. 55)

1 lime, quartered

cilantro, chopped (for garnish)

1. In large stockpot, heat oil over medium heat. Add onions, red pepper, garlic, and jalapeño. Cook until soft, about 4 minutes.

2. Add chicken broth, coconut milk, tomatoes, chicken, carrots, cilantro, brown sugar, salt, and pepper.

3. Cook on medium-low heat until carrots are tender, about 10 minutes.

4. Garnish with Tortilla Strips, lime, and cilantro.

Hungarian Beef and Potato Soup

SERVES 12

This beef and potato soup is a favorite with boys and men. If you have a meat-and-potato lover in your home, try this simple recipe.

1 cup chopped onion

1 cup chopped green bell pepper

2 Tbsp. olive oil

1 lb. lean ground beef

2 Tbsp. flour

3 cups beef broth

3 cups water

2 cups potatoes peeled and cut into ½-inch cubes

1 Tbsp. tomato paste

1 Tbsp. paprika

1 tsp. dried marjoram

1 tsp. caraway seeds

1 tsp. salt

¼ tsp. cayenne pepper

1. In large stockpot over medium heat, cook onion and pepper in oil until soft, about 4 minutes.

2. Add ground beef and cook until browned. Sprinkle flour over mixture and stir.

3. Reduce heat to medium-low. Add broth, water, potatoes, tomato paste, and seasonings.

4. Cook until potatoes are tender, about 10 minutes.

Chicken and Rice Soup

SERVES 12

Like chicken noodle soup, Chicken and Rice Soup is a classic recipe both kids and adults can enjoy, especially when it's cold outside. This is a warm, homey, comfort soup.

2 Tbsp. canola oil

1 cup diced onion

1 cup peeled and diced carrots

¾ cup diced celery

3 cloves garlic, minced

3 (15-oz.) cans chicken broth

2 tsp. dried basil

½ tsp. salt

½ tsp. fresh ground pepper

1 pint half-and-half

1 cup frozen peas

2 cups cooked rice

3 cups shredded cooked chicken

1. In large stockpot, heat oil on medium heat. Add onion, carrots, celery, and garlic. Cook until vegetables are tender, about 8 minutes.

2. Add chicken broth, basil, salt, and pepper. Turn heat to medium-low and cook for 10 minutes.

3. Add half-and-half, peas, rice, and chicken. Heat until cooked through, about 4 minutes.

4. Serve immediately.

Two-Bean Chili

SERVES 8

Who doesn't love chili on a cold winter evening? Two-Bean Chili is rustic, hardy, and tasty.

1 lb. lean ground beef

¾ cup diced onion

½ cup diced green pepper

1 Tbsp. canola oil

1 (28-oz.) can stewed tomatoes

1 (14-oz.) can black beans, rinsed and drained

1 (14-oz.) can pinto beans, rinsed and drained

1 (7-oz.) can tomato sauce

1 Tbsp. chili powder

½ Tbsp. cumin

½ tsp. salt

½ tsp. black pepper

saltine crackers

cheese, grated

sour cream

- -

1. In large skillet, brown hamburger.

2. In another skillet, cook onions and green pepper in oil over medium heat until soft.

3. In large stockpot, combine cooked beef, cooked onion, cooked green pepper, tomatoes, beans, tomato sauce, chili powder, cumin, salt, and black pepper.

4. Cook on medium-low heat for 15 minutes.

5. Serve with crackers, cheese, and sour cream.

South-of-the-Border Soup

SERVES 12

I love southwest flavors, and I could eat this every day no matter the season.

2 Tbsp. olive oil

1 cup chopped onion

2 cloves garlic, minced

1 Tbsp. seeded and minced jalapeño pepper

2 cups chicken broth

2 (15-oz.) cans lime and cilantro stewed tomatoes, undrained

3 cups shredded cooked chicken

1 (15-oz.) can corn, drained

1 (15-oz.) can black beans, rinsed and drained

¼ cup lime juice

⅛ cup cilantro, washed and chopped

1½ cups cooked rice

sour cream

guacamole

colby and monterey jack cheese, shredded

1. In large stockpot, heat oil over medium heat. Add onion, garlic, and pepper. Cook until tender, about 4 minutes.

2. Add chicken broth, tomatoes, chicken, corn, beans, lime juice, cilantro, and rice. Cook until heated through, about 5 minutes.

3. Serve with sour cream, guacamole, and shredded cheese.

Cheeseburger Soup

SERVES 10

If you like cheeseburgers, give this soup a try. It is filling, and kids love it. Talk about fast food made at home.

2 Tbsp. olive oil

¾ cup chopped onion

½ cup chopped celery

½ lb. lean ground beef

3 cups beef broth

1 cup potatoes peeled and chopped into 1-inch chunks

½ cup peeled and chopped carrots

1 tsp. dried basil leaves

1 tsp. dried parsley leaves

4 Tbsp. butter

¼ cup flour

1½ cups milk

¼ cup sour cream

2 cups Velveeta cheese, cubed

1. In large stockpot, heat oil over medium heat. Add onions and celery and cook until tender, about 4 minutes.

2. Add beef and brown, about 6 minutes. Add broth, potatoes, carrots, and seasonings. Cook for 10 minutes, or until tender.

3. In saucepan, melt butter. Add flour and cook until thickened. Add milk all at once.

4. Add milk mixture to stockpot and stir to combine.

5. Turn heat to medium-low and add sour cream and cheese. Cook until cheese is melted, about 4 minutes. Do not boil.

Chinese Chicken Noodle Soup

SERVES 4

Chicken noodle soup is found in many different cultures, each with their own unique and wonderful variation of flavors and ingredients. This soup incorporates three flavorings often found in Chinese cuisine: ginger, garlic, and green onions.

1 Tbsp. peanut oil

2 cloves garlic, minced

½ Tbsp. grated fresh ginger

2 (15-oz.) cans chicken broth

1 Tbsp. soy sauce

½ Tbsp. red chili sauce

2 green onions, thinly sliced

6 oz. rice noodles

2 cups shredded cooked chicken

½ tsp. fresh ground black pepper

2 cups baby spinach, washed and dried

- -

1. In large stockpot, heat oil, garlic, and ginger over medium heat until tender, about 1 minute.

2. Add chicken broth, soy sauce, chili sauce, and green onions. Bring to a boil.

3. Turn heat to medium-low. Add noodles and cook until tender, about 7 minutes.

4. Add chicken and black pepper. Simmer for 3 minutes.

5. Just before serving, add spinach.

CASSEROLES

67 Chicken and Rice Casserole

68 Chicken and Stuffing Bake

69 Chicken Divan

70 Chicken Noodle Casserole

72 Shepherd's Pie

73 Tater Tot Casserole

74 Tamale Pie

76 Chicken Enchiladas

Chicken and Rice Casserole

SERVES 12

This casserole is likely the most popular casserole made for new mothers, likely due to the fact that families love this comfort food with its mild flavor.

1 Tbsp. olive oil

¾ cup diced onion

2 cloves garlic, minced

½ cup chicken broth

½ cup sour cream

¼ cup cream

1 tsp. Italian seasonings

1 tsp. poultry seasoning

½ tsp. paprika

½ tsp. salt

½ tsp. pepper

1 cup long-grain white rice, cooked

3 cups shredded cooked chicken

1. Preheat oven to 375 degrees.

2. In large skillet, heat oil on medium-high heat. Add onion and garlic. Cook until tender, about 4 minutes.

3. Add chicken broth, sour cream, cream, and seasonings. Simmer for 5 minutes.

4. In 9 × 13 baking dish, add rice, chicken, and cream mixture.

5. Bake for 15 minutes.

Chicken and Stuffing Bake

SERVES 12

This recipe is savory and delicious. It's like Thanksgiving in a dish. Pair it with cranberry relish and you have a perfect "man dish."

4 Tbsp. butter

¼ cup flour

2 cups whole milk

½ tsp. thyme leaves

¼ tsp. celery salt

¼ tsp. pepper

¼ tsp. salt

½ cup sour cream

3 cups shredded cooked chicken

1 cup frozen peas

1 (6-oz.) pkg. stuffing mix, prepared according to directions

cranberry relish

1. Preheat oven to 350 degrees.

2. Melt butter in a medium saucepan over medium heat. Add flour and stir until mixture thickens, about 2 minutes.

3. Add milk all at once followed by seasonings. Stir until thick, about 3 minutes.

4. Turn heat down to low and add sour cream followed by chicken and peas.

5. Evenly pour chicken mixture in a greased 8 × 8 baking dish, followed by prepared stuffing.

6. Bake for 10 minutes, or until bubbly around edges.

7. Serve with cranberry relish.

Chicken Divan

SERVES 10

Men and kids love this healthy and hardy comfort dish. It is always nice to sneak in a leafy green vegetable for flavor, color, and nutrition.

3 cups cooked chicken shredded or cut into 1-inch cubes (I use a cooked rotisserie chicken)

3 cups broccoli florets broken into 1-inch pieces and steamed until tender

1 (10.75-oz.) can cream of chicken soup

1 Tbsp. butter, melted

½ cup mayonnaise or plain yogurt

¼ tsp. curry powder

1 cup shredded mild cheddar cheese

½ cup seasoned bread crumbs

1. Preheat oven to 350 degrees.

2. In medium bowl, combine chicken, broccoli, soup, butter, mayonnaise or yogurt, and curry powder.

3. Spread chicken mixture in greased 9 × 13 dish.

4. Spread cheese evenly over chicken mixture, then repeat with bread crumbs.

5. Bake for 25 minutes.

Note: This dish freezes well—cook once, eat twice.

Chicken Noodle Casserole

SERVES 12

This casserole is creamy, savory, and a little sophisticated.

6 Tbsp. butter, divided

¼ cup flour

4 cups whole milk

1 cup sour cream

½ tsp. salt

½ tsp. black pepper

12 oz. egg noodles

1 cup panko bread crumbs

2 cups shredded cooked chicken

½ cup baby spinach washed, dried, and chopped into 1-inch pieces

2 tsp. dried thyme leaves

1. In large saucepan over medium heat, melt 4 tablespoons of butter. Add flour and stir until foamy.

2. Whisk in milk. Reduce heat to medium-low and cook until mixture thickens, about 4 minutes.

3. Remove from heat and whisk in sour cream, salt, and pepper.

4. Cook noodles in boiling water until tender, about 8 minutes. Drain.

5. In small bowl in microwave, melt 2 tablespoons of butter. Add panko crumbs and stir to coat. Set aside. Add milk mixture, chicken, spinach, and thyme to the pot of drained noodles and stir.

6. Transfer mixture to 9 × 13 greased baking dish. Evenly sprinkle with bread crumbs. Bake in 400-degree oven until bread crumbs are golden, about 10 minutes.

Shepherd's Pie

SERVES 10

Home cooks have been making this dish for centuries because it calls for "leftover" ingredients, which creates a homey, tasty pie that satisfies hungry families.

1 Tbsp. olive oil

¾ cup diced onion

2 cloves garlic, minced

1½ lbs. lean ground beef

1 tsp. salt

½ tsp. pepper

2 Tbsp. flour

2 tsp. tomato paste

1 cup beef broth

1 tsp. worcestershire sauce

1 tsp. dried rosemary

¼ tsp. dried thyme

½ cup frozen corn kernels

½ cup frozen peas

3 cups mashed potatoes (leftovers work well, or instant potatoes)

½ cup shredded mild cheddar cheese

1. In large skillet, heat oil over medium heat. Add onion and garlic. Cook until tender, about 4 minutes. Add beef, salt, and pepper. Cook until beef is browned, about 5 minutes. Sprinkle flour over beef.

2. Add tomato paste, beef broth, worcestershire sauce, rosemary, and thyme. Simmer for 10 minutes. Add corn and peas.

3. In 9 × 13 dish, spread meat mixture on bottom. Spread mashed potatoes evenly over meat mixture. Sprinkle with cheese.

4. Bake in 400-degree oven for 10 minutes, or until cheese is melted and pie is heated through.

Tater Tot Casserole

SERVES 10

Tater Tots are one of kids' favorite foods. When you add meat in a flavorful cream sauce and cheese, this becomes a family-favorite meal as well.

1½ lbs. lean ground beef

1 (10.75-oz.) can cream of mushroom soup

½ cup sour cream

½ tsp. celery seeds

½ tsp. salt

½ tsp. black pepper

1½ cups shredded colby jack cheese, divided

1 (16-oz.) pkg. frozen Tater Tots

1. Preheat oven to 375 degrees.

2. In large skillet, brown beef on medium heat, about 6 minutes.

3. In medium bowl, combine soup, sour cream, celery seeds, salt, and pepper.

4. Add soup mixture to meat mixture and stir to combine.

5. Spread meat mixture in greased 9 × 13 baking dish, followed by 1 cup cheese.

6. Layer Tater Tots and remaining cheese over meat mixture.

7. Bake for 20 minutes.

Tamale Pie

SERVES 12

If you are anything like me, making tamales is intimidating. However, this is a simple way to get the tamale taste with the ease of making a tasty Mexican casserole.

1½ cups lean ground beef

1 Tbsp. canola oil

¾ cup diced onions

½ cup diced green pepper

1 (15-oz.) can Mexican-style diced tomatoes, undrained

1 cup frozen corn

1 Tbsp. chili powder

½ tsp. salt

½ tsp. pepper

½ cup olives, sliced

Tamale Topping (see next page)

1. Preheat oven to 375 degrees.

2. In large skillet, brown beef on medium heat for about 6 minutes. Transfer to plate and cover.

3. In same skillet, heat oil over medium heat. Add onions and green pepper. Cook until tender, about 4 minutes.

4. Add browned beef, tomatoes, corn, chili powder, salt, pepper, and olives to skillet.

5. Cook on medium-low heat for 5 minutes.

6. Put mixture in bottom of greased 9 × 13 baking dish.

7. Spread Tamale Topping evenly over meat mixture. Bake for 20 minutes.

Tamale Topping

2 cups milk

2 Tbsp. butter

1 tsp. salt

1 cup cornmeal

1. In medium saucepan, heat milk, butter, and salt over medium-low heat.

2. Slowly stir in cornmeal and cook until mixture thickens, about 1 minute.

Chicken Enchiladas

SERVES 8

This is a classic and tasty chicken enchilada recipe with a white, creamy sauce.

1 Tbsp. olive oil

½ cup finely chopped onion

3 cups shredded cooked chicken

1 (10.75-oz.) can cream of chicken soup

½ cup sour cream

½ cup chicken broth

1 (4-oz.) can diced green chilies

1 (4-oz.) can black olives, sliced

2 cups shredded monterey jack cheese, divided

8 (8-inch) flour tortillas

1. Preheat oven to 350 degrees.

2. In small skillet, heat oil over medium heat. Add onion and cook until tender, about 4 minutes.

3. In medium bowl, combine chicken, onion, soup, sour cream, chicken broth, green chilies, and olives.

4. Fold in 1 cup shredded cheese.

5. Spread ½ cup chicken mixture down center of each tortilla, leaving an inch on each end.

6. Place tortillas in greased 9 × 13 baking dish. Evenly spread remaining cheese over top.

7. Bake for 20 minutes.

PASTAS

78 Bow-Tie Carbonara

79 Asparagus, Chicken, and Mushroom Fettuccine

80 Rigatoni Bolognese

81 Lemon Chicken Spaghetti

82 Macaroni and Cheese

84 Pomodoro Sauce and Spaghetti

85 Stuffed Manicotti Shells

86 Cheese Ravioli with Creamy Marinara

87 Garlic Bread

88 Penne Pasta with Tomato Cream Sauce

89 Spaghetti with Ragù Sauce

91 Light Alfredo and Fettuccine

Bow-Tie Carbonara

SERVES 8

Are you looking for an inexpensive and quick pasta recipe? Then you have found it with Bow-Tie Carbonara. This recipe can be made in minutes. The smoky bacon flavor and cheese make this dish delicious.

1 (16-oz.) pkg. mini bow-tie pasta

4 Tbsp. butter

¾ cup grated parmesan cheese

2 eggs, beaten

½ tsp. fresh ground pepper

¼ tsp. salt

½ cup frozen peas, thawed under cool water and drained

¼ cup peeled and shredded carrots

⅓ cup chopped fresh parsley

1 lb. bacon, cooked crisp and crumbled

----

1. Cook pasta in salted boiling water for 7 minutes, or until tender.

2. Drain pasta and turn heat to low.

3. Add butter and stir until melted.

4. Combine parmesan cheese and eggs in a bowl. Add to pasta mixture. Stir until eggs are cooked and cheese is melted, about 2 minutes.

5. Sprinkle with pepper and salt. Add peas, carrots, parsley, and bacon. Fold to combine.

6. Serve immediately.

Asparagus, Chicken, and Mushroom Fettuccine

SERVES 8

Sun-dried tomatoes and asparagus offer this dish outstanding flavor and beautiful color. This is a delightful cream sauce made lighter with chicken.

¾ lb. mushrooms, washed and sliced

1 clove garlic, minced

¾ cup butter, divided

2 lbs. asparagus, washed and cut into 2-inch pieces

1 cup grilled chicken strips

½ cup sun-dried tomatoes

1 cup cream

1 lb. fettuccine, cooked tender

1 cup shredded parmesan cheese

⅓ cup chopped fresh parsley

- -

1. In larger skillet, sauté mushrooms and garlic in ¼ cup butter over medium-high heat for 2 minutes.

2. Add asparagus, grilled chicken, tomatoes, cream, and remaining butter. Bring to a boil. Reduce to simmer and cook for 3 minutes.

3. Add hot fettuccine, parmesan cheese, and parsley to skillet and toss.

4. Serve immediately.

Rigatoni Bolognese

SERVES 8

What is it about pasta that grown-ups and kids both love? Maybe it's the fun pasta shapes and textures, or maybe it's the interesting and varied sauces and Italian cheeses that make pasta dishes so good. Rigatoni Bolognese is definitely one of my favorite pasta and sauce combinations.

1 lb. lean ground beef

2 Tbsp. olive oil

¾ cup diced onion

½ cup diced green bell pepper

1 carrot, peeled and shredded

42 oz. canned crushed tomatoes, undrained

½ cup apple juice

2 tsp. dried oregano

2 tsp. dried basil

1 tsp. dried thyme

1 tsp. garlic powder

1 bay leaf

½ tsp. salt

½ tsp. fresh ground pepper

10 oz. rigatoni pasta, cooked tender (about 9 minutes)

½ cup fresh grated parmesan cheese

- -

1. In medium skillet, brown beef over medium heat for about 6 minutes. Remove from pan and set aside.

2. In same skillet, heat olive oil. Add onion, pepper, and carrot. Cook until tender, about 4 minutes.

3. Stir in crushed tomatoes, apple juice, oregano, basil, thyme, garlic powder, bay leaf, salt, and pepper.

4. Bring to a boil, and then simmer for 15 minutes. Stir in browned hamburger.

5. Serve over cooked rigatoni pasta. Sprinkle with parmesan cheese before serving.

Lemon Chicken Spaghetti

SERVES 8

This light pasta is lovely paired with a garden salad in the summer and spring.

2 Tbsp. olive oil

2 cloves garlic, minced

4 chicken breasts, trimmed and cut into 1-inch strips

4 Tbsp. butter

3 Tbsp. fresh lemon juice

½ tsp. dried oregano

½ tsp. black pepper

1 (14.5-oz.) can chicken broth

2 Tbsp. cornstarch

1 lb. spaghetti noodles, cooked tender

2 Tbsp. fresh parsley

- -

1. In a large skillet, heat oil over medium heat. Add garlic and stir 1 minute.

2. Add chicken strips and cook for about 8 minutes, turning once.

3. Remove chicken from skillet and set aside.

4. In same skillet, melt butter. Add lemon juice, oregano, and black pepper.

5. In separate bowl, combine broth and cornstarch, stirring until cornstarch is completely dissolved.

6. Add to skillet, and add chicken strips. Simmer until sauce thickens.

7. Toss with hot pasta and sprinkle with parsley.

Macaroni and Cheese

SERVES 12

Boxed mac and cheese does not hold a candle to this dish. This is comfort food at its finest and a child pleaser to say the least. One winter afternoon, I made it for a bunch of teenagers. One of the boys said, "My dad is a chef, but this is the best macaroni and cheese I have ever tasted!"

¼ cup butter

¼ cup flour

2½ cups milk

½ tsp. salt

1 tsp. black pepper

1 egg, beaten

½ tsp. seasoned salt

1 tsp. dry mustard

1 lb. colby jack cheese, grated

4 cups dried macaroni, cooked for 5 minutes, until firm but tender

1 cup panko bread crumbs

- -

1. Preheat oven to 350 degrees.

2. In saucepan, melt butter. Add flour and stir until bubbly.

3. Add milk and stir until thick. Add salt and pepper.

4. Pour ¼ cup of sauce over egg. Whisk.

5. Pour egg mixture back into remaining milk sauce. Add seasoned salt and dry mustard. Stir. Add cheese. Stir until melted.

6. Put cooked macaroni in large baking dish. Pour cheese mixture over macaroni.

7. Evenly sprinkle bread crumbs over macaroni mixture.

8. Bake for 10 minutes.

Pomodoro Sauce and Spaghetti

SERVES 8

Over the course of several book signings, I asked some of the children what their favorite food was. Spaghetti with red sauce usually made it into the top three foods kids love.

1 Tbsp. olive oil

½ cup chopped onion

3 cloves garlic, minced

1 (28-oz.) can crushed tomatoes

1 (8-oz.) can tomato sauce

2 Tbsp. finely chopped fresh parsley

1 tsp. dried basil leaves

1 tsp. dried oregano leaves

1 tsp. sugar

½ tsp. thyme

½ tsp. fennel seeds

½ tsp. marjoram

16 oz. spaghetti noodles, cooked tender

1. Heat oil in skillet on medium heat. Add onion and garlic, and cook until tender, about 4 minutes.

2. Add tomatoes, tomato sauce, parsley, and seasonings.

3. Simmer on medium-low heat for 15 minutes.

4. Serve over cooked spaghetti.

Stuffed Manicotti Shells

SERVES 12

Stuffed Manicotti Shells are an easy and tasty way to prepare pasta. Kids like the idea of eating a "stuffed shell."

1 (8-oz.) box manicotti shells (14)

8 oz. ricotta cheese

½ cup shredded parmesan cheese

1 Tbsp. dried parsley

½ tsp. salt

½ tsp. fresh ground pepper

3½ cups (32-oz. jar) basil and tomato pasta sauce, divided

2 cups shredded mozzarella cheese

4 fresh basil leaves, chopped

---

1. Preheat oven to 350 degrees.

2. Cook manicotti shells in boiling water for about 7 minutes, or until tender. Drain immediately.

3. Combine ricotta cheese, parmesan cheese, parsley, salt, and pepper.

4. Spoon 2 tablespoons of cheese mixture into each shell.

5. Spread 1 cup of pasta sauce on bottom of 9 × 13 baking dish. Arrange stuffed manicotti in a single layer over sauce. Cover evenly with mozzarella cheese and then remaining sauce.

6. Cover with foil and bake for 20 minutes.

7. Garnish with fresh basil.

Cheese Ravioli with Creamy Marinara

SERVES 4

This is my go-to dinner when I have just minutes to prepare. Bonus: It's really good!

12 frozen four-cheese ravioli (3 per person)

1 lb. bottled tomato and basil marinara

2 Tbsp. whipping cream

4 basil leaves, chopped

2 Tbsp. black olives, sliced

2 Tbsp. finely shredded fresh parmesan cheese

- -

1. In large stockpot, bring salted water to boil.

2. Place frozen ravioli in water and cook until ravioli are floating, about 5 minutes. Drain.

3. In separate saucepan, add marinara, whipping cream, and basil leaves. Heat through, about 4 minutes.

4. Spoon sauce over ravioli and sprinkle with olives and parmesan cheese.

Garlic Bread

SERVES 12

This easy-to-make buttery bread makes a perfect accompaniment to any pasta or Italian meal.

8 Tbsp. butter, melted

½ tsp. garlic powder

1 loaf French bread, cut in half lengthwise (horizontally)

1 Tbsp. dried parsley

½ tsp. paprika

⅛ cup fresh grated parmesan cheese

- -

1. In small bowl, combine butter and garlic powder. Place cut bread on cookie sheet.

2. Using a pastry brush, spread butter mixture over each French bread half.

3. Evenly sprinkle dried parsley and paprika over buttered halves.

4. Evenly spread cheese over buttered halves.

5. Broil on low until cheese is melted and edges are golden brown, about 3 minutes.

6. Cut into 2-inch slices and serve hot.

Note: Leave the door of the oven open when broiling to keep an eye on the bread and keep it from burning.

Penne Pasta with Tomato Cream Sauce

SERVES 10

This simple Italian recipe can be made in a snap for lunch or dinner.

2 cups tomato and basil pasta sauce

½ cup whipping cream

½ cup fresh basil leaves

8 oz. penne pasta, cooked tender

⅓ cup grated parmesan cheese

- -

1. In medium saucepan over medium-low heat, warm pasta sauce, whipping cream, and basil leaves.

2. Transfer warm cooked pasta to a large bowl. Add cream sauce and toss to coat.

3. Sprinkle with parmesan cheese and serve immediately.

Spaghetti with Ragù Sauce

SERVES 8

Have you noticed that spaghetti with ragù sauce is on most kid's menus at restaurants? This is because kids love it. The noodles are fun to roll on a fork, and the ragù sauce lends color, flavor, and nutrition. This is a win-win recipe.

1 Tbsp. olive oil

½ cup diced green peppers

2 cloves garlic, minced

1 lb. lean ground beef

1 (32-oz.) can crushed tomatoes

1 tsp. dried oregano

1 tsp. dried basil

3 tsp. dried parsley

½ tsp. dried thyme

½ tsp. salt

½ tsp. black pepper

½ tsp. sugar

1 lb. spaghetti noodles, cooked tender

½ cup fresh grated parmesan cheese

- -

1. In skillet over medium heat, add olive oil, green peppers, and garlic. Cook until tender, about 4 minutes.

2. Add ground beef to skillet and cook until browned.

3. Add tomatoes, oregano, basil, parsley, thyme, salt, black pepper, and sugar. Simmer meat mixture for 10 minutes.

4. Serve meat sauce over cooked spaghetti noodles. Garnish with parmesan cheese.

Light Alfredo and Fettuccine

SERVES 10

Kids love alfredo. However, I have found that most alfredo recipes are too rich and fattening for my personal taste. In my opinion, this is the perfect consistency and creaminess.

2 Tbsp. butter

3 cloves garlic, minced

1 tsp. lemon zest

1 Tbsp. flour

1 cup 2% milk

2 Tbsp. cream cheese

1 cup shredded parmesan cheese

¼ tsp. salt

¼ tsp. white pepper

2 Tbsp. chopped fresh parsley

12 oz. fettuccine noodles, cooked tender

- -

1. In a medium saucepan, melt butter. Add garlic and lemon zest.

2. Cook for 1 minute over medium heat.

3. Add flour and stir. Add milk and stir well.

4. Add cream cheese, parmesan cheese, salt, and white pepper. Stir.

5. Add parsley and toss alfredo sauce with fettuccine noodles. Serve immediately.

CHICKEN

93 Basil Butter Chicken

94 Savory Chicken Squares

95 Chicken Fajitas

96 Chicken Taquitos

98 Sweet and Sour Chicken

99 Honey Mustard Chicken

100 Popcorn Chicken

103 Hawaiian Haystacks

104 Chicken Parmesan

105 Chicken Nuggets

106 Cheese and Chicken Quesadillas

108 Teriyaki Chicken

Basil Butter Chicken

SERVES 4

This is a delicious, savory chicken recipe. Everything tastes better with butter; chicken is no exception.

½ tsp. salt

½ tsp. pepper

4 chicken breasts, quartered

⅓ cup butter, melted

¼ cup chopped fresh basil

½ cup butter, softened

2 Tbsp. minced fresh basil

1 Tbsp. grated parmesan cheese

¼ tsp. garlic powder

⅛ tsp. salt

⅛ tsp. pepper

1. Sprinkle ½ teaspoon salt and ½ teaspoon pepper on chicken.

2. Combine ⅓ cup melted butter and ¼ cup chopped basil. Stir. Brush chicken with melted butter mixture.

3. In separate bowl, combine softened butter, minced basil, parmesan cheese, garlic powder, ⅛ teaspoon of salt, and ⅛ teaspoon of pepper. Beat until smooth. Set basil-butter mixture aside.

4. Grill chicken over medium coals for 8–10 minutes on each side, basting frequently with remaining melted butter mixture.

5. Serve grilled chicken with basil-butter mixture.

Savory Chicken Squares

SERVES 8

This savory dish is divine. It is elegant, yet kids love it. It also packs well for school lunches the next day. Your child will be the envy of the students and teachers in the cafeteria. Don't forget Dad: the men at the office will definitely want to trade.

3 cups shredded cooked chicken

8 oz. cream cheese, softened

1 Tbsp. milk

3 green onions, sliced thin

1 Tbsp. pimientos

½ tsp. garlic powder

¼ tsp. black pepper

2 (7-oz.) pkgs. refrigerated crescent rolls

¾ cup butter, melted

1 cup seasoned croutons, crushed

1. In large bowl, combine chicken, cream cheese, and milk. Stir until well incorporated. Add onions, pimientos, garlic powder, and pepper to cream cheese mixture. Stir to blend.

2. Separate crescent rolls and roll each out into a 5-inch square.

3. In the center of each square, add ¼ cup of chicken mixture.

4. Bring up each end of the square to the center, overlapping by ½ inch to seal.

5. Brush each chicken square with butter and then roll in crushed croutons.

6. Bake in 350-degree oven for 20 minutes, or until crescent dough is golden brown.

Note: Freezes well—cook once, eat twice.

Chicken Fajitas

SERVES 6

Hands down, when I dine at Mexican restaurants, I order chicken fajitas. Even as a grown-up, it is fun to fill my own flour tortilla with my favorite accompaniments. Now you can serve these at home.

3 Tbsp. olive oil

2 Tbsp. fresh lime juice

¼ cup finely chopped fresh cilantro

1 Tbsp. seeded and minced jalapeño pepper

1 tsp. ground cumin

1 tsp. dried oregano

1 tsp. chili powder

½ tsp. garlic powder

½ tsp. black pepper

2 lbs. boneless chicken, cut into ½-inch strips

1 Tbsp. olive oil

½ red bell pepper, sliced thin

½ green bell pepper, sliced thin

½ cup thinly sliced red onion

1 tomato, sliced thin

6 (8-inch) flour tortillas

sour cream, shredded mild cheddar cheese, guacamole, sliced black olives

1. In glass bowl, combine oil, lime juice, cilantro, jalapeño, cumin, oregano, chili powder, garlic powder, and black pepper. Add chicken and let marinate for 20 minutes. In large skillet, heat 1 tablespoon oil over medium-high heat. Add bell peppers, red onion, and tomato. Cook until tender, about 5 minutes. Remove from heat and cover.

2. In same skillet, add chicken removed from marinade. Cook, turning several times, for about 6 minutes, or until largest piece is no longer pink. Return peppers, onion, and tomato to skillet and heat through, about 2 minutes. Divide fajita mixture among tortillas and garnish with sour cream, cheese, guacamole, and olives.

Chicken Taquitos

SERVES 8

No need to reach for taquitos in the frozen food section with this quick, easy, and tasty recipe on hand. After sinking your teeth in one of these amazingly good taquitos, that frozen food section will be a thing of the past.

2 cups shredded cooked chicken

½ cup fire-roasted tomato and corn salsa

½ cup sour cream

½ cup canned black beans, rinsed and drained

½ tsp. cumin

½ tsp. salt

½ tsp. pepper

1 cup shredded colby jack cheese

8 (8-inch) flour tortillas

salsa

1. Preheat oven to 425 degrees.

2. In medium bowl, combine chicken, salsa, sour cream, beans, cumin, salt, pepper, and cheese.

3. Spread ½ cup chicken filling on lower third of each tortilla, leaving 1 inch on sides.

4. From filling side, roll each tortilla tight and place seam side down on cookie sheet.

5. Spray tortillas with cooking spray.

6. Bake for 8–10 minutes, or until beginning to brown.

7. Serve with salsa.

Sweet and Sour Chicken

SERVES 6

Recipes that incorporate sweet and savory flavors and ingredients rate high with me. Here is one such recipe that is sure to please.

1 Tbsp. butter

1 Tbsp. canola oil

3 chicken breasts, cut into 1-inch chunks

½ cup ketchup

½ cup soy sauce

½ cup brown sugar

¼ cup pineapple juice (reserved from can, below)

1 clove garlic, minced

½ cup diced green pepper

½ cup canned pineapple tidbits, drained and liquid reserved

3 cups cooked rice

- -

1. In large skillet, heat butter and oil over medium heat.

2. Add chicken and brown on each side, about 8 minutes.

3. In small bowl, combine ketchup, soy sauce, brown sugar, pineapple juice, and garlic. Pour sauce over chicken. Add green pepper and pineapple tidbits.

4. Cook over medium-low heat until chicken is no longer pink, about 8 minutes.

5. Serve over cooked rice.

Honey Mustard Chicken

SERVES 4

Chicken and honey mustard are particularly complementary. The honey mustard gives this dish a sweet and tangy flavor.

⅔ cup dijon mustard

⅔ cup honey

2 tsp. apple cider vinegar

½ tsp. salt

½ tsp. black pepper

1 Tbsp. olive oil

1 Tbsp. butter

2 cloves garlic, minced

2 lbs. chicken tender pieces
   (½-inch thick and 2 inches wide)

- -

1. Preheat oven to 350 degrees.

2. In small bowl, combine mustard, honey, apple cider vinegar, salt, and pepper.

3. In large skillet over medium heat, heat oil and butter until melted.

4. Add garlic and chicken tenders. Cook on each side for 2 minutes to pan sear.

5. Transfer chicken to an 8 × 8 baking dish in a single layer and pour honey-mustard sauce evenly over chicken.

6. Bake for about 15 minutes, or until chicken is no longer pink.

Popcorn Chicken

SERVES 4

This is a fun and unique recipe to make at home. Scoop them in brown paper cones and serve with a variety of dipping sauces and dinner will feel like a night at the fair.

4 chicken breasts

2 cups buttermilk

1 Tbsp. dried rosemary

2 cups flour

1 tsp. garlic powder

1 tsp. salt

1 tsp. black pepper

½ tsp. paprika

canola oil for frying

- -

1. Cut chicken breasts into 1-inch cubes.

2. In a resealable gallon bag, soak chicken breasts in buttermilk mixed with rosemary for 15–20 minutes.

3. In another resealable gallon bag, combine flour, garlic powder, salt, pepper, and paprika.

4. Add chicken to flour mixture and shake to coat.

5. Heat 5 inches of oil in large stockpot. Bring to 375 degrees.

6. Using a slotted spoon, ease flour-coated chicken into oil.

7. Cook until golden and cooked through, about 4 minutes.

8. Serve with honey mustard, ranch dressing, or barbecue sauce.

Chicken
Hawaiian Haystacks

SERVES 8

Whenever children have a hand in assembling their food, the propensity to like the dish goes up. Hawaiian haystacks is an appropriate name for a meal that gets better the more you pile on.

2 (15-oz.) cans cream of chicken soup

1 (15-oz.) can chicken broth

3 cups shredded cooked chicken

4 cups cooked rice

Toppings:

chow mein noodles

shredded coconut

pineapple tidbits

green onions, thinly sliced

sweet bell pepper, diced

water chestnuts, diced

celery, diced

mild cheddar cheese, shredded

- -

1. In large saucepan, mix soup and broth, and bring to a simmer. Add chicken and cook on low heat for 8 minutes.

2. Ladle ½ cup chicken mixture over ½ cup cooked rice for each haystack.

3. Add favorite toppings.

Chicken Parmesan

SERVES 8

Chicken parmesan is something I often order at Italian restaurants. But there's no need to dine out to enjoy this wonderful Italian dish; it's easy to prepare at home.

4 chicken breasts, cut in half horizontally (about ½ inch thick)

1 cup seasoned bread crumbs

¾ cup grated parmesan cheese, divided

2 Tbsp. dried parsley

1 tsp. garlic powder

½ tsp. salt

⅛ tsp. pepper

½ cup butter, melted

1 lb. spaghetti, cooked tender

spaghetti sauce of choice

- -

1. Preheat oven to 350 degrees.

2. Between 2 sheets of wax paper, pound chicken breast halves to ¼-inch thickness.

3. In medium bowl, combine bread crumbs, ½ cup of parmesan cheese, parsley, garlic powder, salt, and pepper.

4. Dip chicken into melted butter and then into crumb mixture. Coat well.

5. In 9 × 13 shallow baking dish, arrange chicken in a single layer. Sprinkle remaining cheese evenly over chicken.

6. Bake for 15 minutes, or until no longer pink in center.

7. Serve over cooked spaghetti and sauce.

Chicken Nuggets

SERVES 4

Most of us buy chicken nuggets at fast-food chains. However, this is a great fast food to make in your own kitchen.

4 chicken breasts, cut into fourths

1 cup buttermilk

4 dashes hot sauce

6 cups canola oil

1 cup flour

1 tsp. garlic powder

1 tsp. onion powder

1 tsp. salt

½ tsp. baking soda

½ tsp. black pepper

½ tsp. dried thyme

½ tsp. paprika

2 eggs

1½ Tbsp. water

- -

1. In resealable gallon bag, add chicken, buttermilk, and hot sauce. Let soak for 20 minutes. In large stockpot, heat oil to 375 degrees.

2. In small bowl, combine flour, garlic powder, onion powder, salt, baking soda, pepper, thyme, and paprika. Place mixture in shallow dish.

3. In another shallow bowl, whisk together eggs and water.

4. Take handful of chicken and dip in egg mixture followed by dredging in flour mixture. Immediately drop in hot oil. Repeat for all chicken pieces.

5. Cook for 6 minutes, or until chicken is no longer pink. Serve with ketchup, honey mustard, barbecue sauce, ranch dressing, or other favorite dipping sauce.

Cheese and Chicken Quesadillas

SERVES 4

If you need to get dinner done in minutes, then consider making Cheese and Chicken Quesadillas for dinner. The recipe calls for few ingredients and cooks up in a flash. This is a simple but satisfying meal.

butter

8 (8-inch) flour tortillas

1 cup shredded monterey jack cheese

1 cup shredded pepper jack cheese

2 cups shredded cooked chicken

½ cup sour cream

2 Tbsp. fresh cilantro

1 cup Fresh Salsa (see next page)

¼ cup sliced black olives

8 avocado slices, or guacamole

- -

1. In skillet with a teaspoon of butter, place flour tortilla.

2. Add ½ cup mixed cheeses and ½ cup chicken, and top with another flour tortilla.

3. Cook, turning once, until golden brown on each side. Repeat steps for all quesadillas.

4. In a small bowl, combine sour cream and cilantro.

5. Top each quesadilla with ¼ cup salsa, ⅛ cup sour cream with cilantro, 1 tablespoon olives, and 2 avocado slices (or guacamole).

Fresh Salsa --

This is a quick and easy salsa recipe, and it's a perfect garnish for Mexican dishes or egg burritos. Serves 12.

2 medium tomatoes, seeded and chopped

¼ cup chopped red onion

¼ cup fresh cilantro leaves, chopped

1 clove garlic, finely chopped

juice of 1 lime

1 Tbsp. olive oil

½ tsp. salt

½ tsp. pepper

1. In a medium bowl, combine all ingredients.

Teriyaki Chicken

SERVES 6

Here is another family-favorite ethnic dish. It is quick and packed with flavors of the orient.

1 lb. chicken breasts, cut into ½-inch strips

2 Tbsp. canola or peanut oil

1 tsp. crushed garlic

1 bunch green onions, chopped

1 Tbsp. peeled and minced fresh ginger

3 Tbsp. granulated sugar

2 Tbsp. cornstarch

½ cup chicken broth

3 Tbsp. soy sauce

rice

Tempura Vegetables (see next page)

- -

1. In hot skillet, sear chicken in oil on medium-high heat. Brown all pieces. Add garlic, green onions, and ginger. Stir-fry for 1 minute. Continue to cook chicken on medium heat.

2. In separate bowl, combine sugar, cornstarch, chicken broth, and soy sauce. Whisk until combined. Add to chicken in skillet. Cook until chicken is no longer pink.

3. Serve over rice with Tempura Vegetables.

Tempura Vegetables ------------------------------

Tempura Vegetables are a tasty accompaniment to any Asian dish. They are surprisingly easy to make. Serves 6.

3 carrots, peeled

1 small zucchini

1 onion

tempura mix (found in Asian section of super market)

2 cups oil

1. Julienne carrots and zucchini. Slice onion. Make tempura according to package directions.

BEEF

111 Garden Burger Sliders

112 Dad's Pepper Steak

113 Navajo Tacos

115 Chalupas

116 Beef and Cheese Enchiladas

119 Beef Stroganoff

120 Bean and Beef Burrito Supreme

123 Hawaiian-Style Meatballs

124 Corn Dogs

127 Beef and Bean Tostadas

Garden Burger Sliders

SERVES 6

Sliders are the rage. They are petite but packed with all the flavor and toppings of a traditional hamburger.

1 lb. lean ground beef

¼ cup diced onion

¼ cup diced green bell pepper

¼ cup diced mushrooms (stems removed)

2 cloves garlic, minced

Special Sauce

(see below)

6 whole wheat dinner rolls

tomatoes, sliced

dill pickles

red onion, sliced thin

iceberg lettuce

----

1. In medium bowl, combine beef, onion, green pepper, mushrooms, and garlic. Fold to combine. Form 6 (4-inch) patties.

2. Grill over medium coals for about 5 minutes each side, or until no longer pink.

3. Make Special Sauce.

4. Assemble slider by spreading sauce over one side of roll. Top with garden patty and favorite vegetable toppings. Top with other side of roll. Repeat for all sliders.

Special Sauce

1 cup mayonnaise

⅓ cup French dressing

¼ cup dill pickle relish

1 tsp. sugar

1. Combine ingredients in small bowl.

Beef
Dad's Pepper Steak

SERVES 8

Pepper steak is a great dish cooked in one pan. The pepper, onion, and spices infuse the steak with great flavor.

2 Tbsp. olive oil

2 bell peppers, sliced thin

½ cup chopped onion

2 cloves garlic, minced

½ cup beef broth

2 Tbsp. soy sauce

1 Tbsp. honey

½ Tbsp. rice vinegar

1½ lbs. flank steak, cut into 3-inch-long and ¼-inch-thick strips

⅛ cup cold water

1 tsp. cornstarch

4 cups cooked rice

1. In large skillet over medium heat, cook oil, peppers, onion, and garlic until tender, about 4 minutes. Remove from skillet.

2. In small bowl, combine beef broth, soy sauce, honey, and vinegar.

3. Add steak to skillet and cook for 10–15 minutes, or until desired doneness.

4. In small bowl, combine water and cornstarch.

5. Add vegetables, beef broth mixture, and water mixture. Cook for another 5 minutes.

6. Serve over cooked rice.

Navajo Tacos

SERVES 8

Fried dough with savory toppings makes this a family-favorite meal. Not to mention it is easy and quick.

1 (16-oz.) pkg. jumbo refrigerator biscuits

½ cup canola oil

2 cups canned chili, warmed

1 cup shredded monterey jack cheese

2 cups shredded lettuce

2 cups chopped tomatoes

½ cup sour cream

½ cup sliced olives

½ cup chopped green onions

1. With a rolling pin, flatten each ball of dough into about a 4-inch square.

2. Heat oil in skillet over medium heat.

3. Cook dough in oil until golden brown on each side.

4. Top each with chili, cheese, lettuce, tomatoes, sour cream, olives, and green onions.

Note: Top extra Navajo Tacos with honey butter for dessert.

Chalupas

SERVES 8

This recipe is a cross between a Navajo taco and a Mexican taco. The fried biscuits lend a chewy texture to the dish piled with traditional taco toppings.

olive oil, for frying

1 (16-oz.) pkg. jumbo refrigerator biscuits

1 lb. lean ground beef

1 (1.75-oz.) pkg. taco seasoning

2 Tbsp. water

1 (15-oz.) can pinto beans, rinsed and drained

- -

Toppings:

2 tomatoes, chopped

2 cups red leaf lettuce chopped into bite-size pieces

1 bunch green onions, chopped

1 cup shredded colby jack cheese

1 cup spicy ranch dressing

½ cup chopped cilantro

- -

1. In large skillet, put ½ inch oil and heat on medium heat. Roll each biscuit into a 5-inch circle. Cook 4 biscuits at a time in skillet until golden brown, about 45 seconds each side.

2. In another large skillet, brown beef on medium heat, about 6 minutes. Add taco seasoning and water to beef and stir until combined. Turn heat to low and cook 1 minute more.

3. Add beans to beef mixture and cook for 4 minutes. Turn off heat and cover to keep warm. Divide meat mixture and toppings among fried biscuits. Fold in half. Serve immediately.

Beef and Cheese Enchiladas

Beef

SERVES 8

Enchiladas are quick and easy. The Mexican tomato sauce adds a wonderful spicy tomato flavor that is mellowed by the cheese and the corn tortillas.

canola oil

8 corn tortillas

1 medium onion, chopped

1 lb. ground beef, browned

1 (5-oz.) can green chilies

1½ cups shredded monterey jack cheese

1 (5-oz.) can Mexican tomato sauce (yellow can in ethnic section of supermarket)

green onions, chopped

½ cup cilantro

½ cup sour cream

---

1. In small skillet, heat ¼ cup oil. Fry each tortilla in hot oil, turning once. This takes about 1 minute per tortilla. Set on paper towels on plate.

2. In about 1 tablespoon of oil in shallow pan, cook onions until tender, about 4 minutes. Add cooked hamburger and green chilies. Stir to combine.

3. To assemble enchiladas, place ⅛ cup beef mixture, 3 tablespoons cheese, and ½–1 tablespoon tomato sauce in each tortilla and fold in half. Place tortillas in 9 × 13 baking dish. When all tortillas are filled, spoon an additional ½ tablespoon of tomato sauce over each filled tortilla.

4. Bake in oven for about 15 minutes, or until cheese is melted. Garnish with green onions, cilantro, and sour cream.

Beef Stroganoff

SERVES 8

Beef stroganoff is another man-pleasing dish. When I ask men what their favorite dishes are, beef stroganoff is often at the top of the list.

1 Tbsp. olive oil

½ cup diced green pepper

½ cup button mushrooms stems removed and sliced

1 lb. sirloin steak, cut into 1-inch chunks

1½ cups whole milk

1 Tbsp. cornstarch

2 Tbsp. dry onion soup mix

1 tsp. dill weed

¼ cup sour cream

4 cups cooked rice (or cooked noodles)

- -

1. In large skillet, heat olive oil over medium heat. Add green pepper and mushrooms. Cook until tender, about 4 minutes. Transfer to plate and cover.

2. Add steak to skillet and brown over medium heat, about 7 minutes.

3. In small bowl, combine milk and cornstarch. Stir until dissolved. Add soup mix, dill weed, and sour cream.

4. Add peppers, mushrooms, and milk mixture to steak and cook over medium-low heat for 5 minutes.

5. Serve over cooked rice or cooked noodles.

Bean and Beef Burrito Supreme

SERVES 4

No need to go to your favorite restaurant the next time you are craving a beef and bean burrito; you can assemble one in a snap at home. This is one of those semi-homemade recipes. Keep in mind that Mexican fast food chains now sell their taco sauce and seasonings in grocery markets.

½ lb. lean ground beef

1 (1-oz.) pkg. taco seasoning mix

2 Tbsp. water

4 (8-inch) flour tortillas

1 cup refried beans

½ cup red taco sauce

1 cup mild cheddar cheese

1 cup shredded lettuce

1 cup diced tomatoes

½ cup sour cream

½ cup sliced olives

1. In large skillet, brown beef over medium heat, about 6 minutes.

2. Add taco seasoning mix and 2 tablespoons water. Stir, cooking on low for 2 minutes. Remove from heat and cover to keep warm.

3. On each flour tortilla, fill center—2 inches from sides—with ¼ cup beans, ⅛ cup taco sauce, 2 tablespoons seasoned beef, and ¼ cup each of cheese, lettuce, and tomatoes. Add 2 tablespoons each of sour cream and olives.

4. Fold in each side followed by each end. Cut in half and serve.

Hawaiian-Style Meatballs

SERVES 8

No question, kids love meatballs. These are sweet and savory and especially good served over rice.

1½ lbs. lean ground beef

¾ cup pineapple chunks (reserve juice)

2 slices French bread, crumbled

1 egg, slightly beaten

½ cup finely chopped onion

2 Tbsp. pineapple juice from can

½ tsp. salt

½ tsp. black pepper

½ cup ketchup

⅓ cup pineapple juice

¼ cup brown sugar

cooked rice

1. Preheat oven to 350 degrees.

2. In medium bowl, combine beef, pineapple, bread, egg, onion, pineapple juice from can, salt, and pepper.

3. Form meat mixture into 16 balls.

4. In small bowl, combine ketchup, ⅓ cup pineapple juice, and brown sugar.

5. In greased 9 × 13 baking dish, place meatballs. Pour sauce evenly over meatballs.

6. Bake for 30 minutes, or until meatballs are no longer pink. Serve over rice.

Corn Dogs

SERVES 4

Corn dogs are not only top sellers at fairs, but they are also a favorite choice for school lunch. Usually, my fourth-grader takes a home lunch, but not on Corn Dog Day. Make corn dogs from scratch and all others will pale in comparison. This blue-ribbon recipe will take you back to the county fair.

6 cups canola oil

¾ cup yellow cornmeal

¾ cup flour, plus more for rolling

2 tsp. baking powder

½ tsp. baking soda

2 tsp. sugar

¼ tsp. salt

¾ cup buttermilk

2 eggs

4 all-beef hot dogs

4 wooden sticks

ketchup

mustard

1. In large stockpot, heat oil to 350 degrees.

2. In medium bowl whisk together cornmeal, flour, baking powder, baking soda, sugar, and salt.

3. In small bowl, combine buttermilk and eggs.

4. Add buttermilk mixture to flour mixture and stir. Batter should be lumpy.

5. Pour batter into a tall 16-ounce glass.

6. Skewer each hot dog with a wooden stick and roll in enough flour to coat each hot dog.

7. Dip floured hot dogs into batter, then immediately put them into the hot oil for 3 minutes, or until hot dogs are golden brown.

8. Serve with ketchup and mustard.

Beef and Bean Tostadas

SERVES 8

Tostadas are just like hard-shell tacos, except they are flat like a disk. So pile the toppings high.

1 lb. lean beef

1 (1-oz.) pkg. taco seasoning, or Taco Seasoning Mix (see below)

2 Tbsp. water

1 cup refried beans

8 corn tostadas

1 cup shredded mild cheddar cheese

1 cup shredded lettuce

1 cup chopped tomatoes

½ cup sour cream

½ cup sliced black olives

1. In large skillet, brown beef over medium heat, about 6 minutes. Add taco seasoning and water, and cook for 2 more minutes. Turn off heat and cover to keep warm.

2. Divide and spread beans among 8 tostadas. Repeat with meat mixture.

3. Divide and top each tostada with cheese, lettuce, tomatoes, sour cream, and black olives.

Taco Seasoning Mix

This lightning-fast recipe for taco seasoning uses ingredients from your spice cabinet.

2 tsp. chili powder

2 tsp. dried oregano

2 tsp. dried onion

¾ tsp. salt

½ tsp. cumin

¼ tsp. cayenne pepper

1. In small bowl, combine all ingredients. Store in airtight container.

FISH

129 Green Onion and Lemon–Crusted Halibut

130 Fish Tacos

132 Lemon and Dill Poached Salmon

134 Lemon Butter Baked Salmon

136 Lemon Garlic Grilled Salmon

139 Fish Sticks with Tartar Sauce

Green Onion and Lemon–Crusted Halibut

SERVES 4

In the 1990s, my dad got this recipe while on a fishing trip to Alaska. We have been making this simple and savory recipe ever since. It is one of our favorite ways to prepare fish, including salmon.

2 lbs. halibut

1 cup mayonnaise

¼ cup finely chopped green onions

2 tsp. lemon pepper

1 lemon, quartered

- -

1. Preheat oven to 350 degrees.

2. Cut halibut into 4 portions and place on 9 × 13 sheet of aluminum foil.

3. In small bowl, combine mayonnaise, green onions, and lemon pepper.

4. Divide and evenly spread green onion topping over halibut portions.

5. Cover with another 9 × 13 sheet of foil. Fold all ends up to seal.

6. Place foil packet on cookie sheet. Bake for 25 minutes, or until halibut flakes with a fork.

7. Serve with lemon wedges.

Fish Tacos

SERVES 8

No need to be on the Mexican coast to enjoy the fresh taste of fish tacos. Using frozen fish sticks makes this a quick and tasty meal any day of the week.

8 (6-inch) white corn tortillas

16 frozen fish sticks, cooked according to package directions, or home cooked

2 cups shredded green cabbage

½ cup Mexican crème

1 cup picante salsa

2 limes, quartered

- -

1. Warm tortillas on microwave-safe plate in microwave for 30 seconds.

2. Fill each tortilla with 2 cooked fish sticks, ¼ cup cabbage, 1 tablespoon crème, and 2 tablespoons salsa.

3. Serve with lime wedges.

Lemon and Dill Poached Salmon

SERVES 4

If you are looking for something light, healthy, and delicious, then you have found it. Lemon and Dill Poached Salmon is moist without using added fat.

2 cups water

½ lemon

1 tsp. dill weed

4 salmon portions

Cucumber Dill Tartar Sauce (see next page)

Sautéed Spinach and Garlic (see next page)

- -

1. In large nonstick skillet, bring water to a boil. Reduce to simmer on medium-low heat.

2. Squeeze juice of lemon half and sprinkle dill weed evenly over salmon portions.

3. Carefully slide salmon portions into simmering water and cook without turning, uncovered, for about 8 minutes, or until salmon flakes with a fork.

4. Serve with Cucumber Dill Tartar Sauce and Sautéed Spinach and Garlic.

Cucumber Dill Tartar Sauce ---------------------------

Inspiration for this fish accompaniment came from Market Street Grill, a gastronomy restaurant. It pairs beautifully with salmon. Serves 4.

¼ cup sour cream

2 Tbsp. mayonnaise

2 Tbsp. peeled and diced
English cucumber

1 Tbsp. fresh lemon juice

1 Tbsp. chopped green onion

1 tsp. dried dill weed

1 clove garlic, minced

1. In small bowl, combine all ingredients.

Sautéed Spinach and Garlic ---------------------

This green leafy vegetable may be the quickest and healthiest side dish on the planet, cooked in less than 4 minutes. Serves 6.

2 Tbsp. olive oil

1 bunch fresh spinach leaves,
washed and dried

4 cloves fresh garlic

½ tsp. salt

½ tsp. fresh cracked black pepper

1. In medium skillet, heat olive oil over medium heat and add spinach, garlic, salt, and pepper.

2. Toss in pan, cooking for about 3 minutes.

Lemon Butter Baked Salmon

SERVES 8

Since salmon is naturally infused with robust flavor, it requires little seasoning to make it taste great. The lemon and butter is all that is needed to complement this tasty, nutritious fish.

3 lbs. salmon

6 Tbsp. butter, melted

juice of 1 lemon

½ tsp. salt

½ tsp. pepper

Golden Encrusted Brussels Sprouts (see next page)

lemon wedges

- -

1. Preheat oven to 400 degrees.

2. Line cookie sheet with aluminum foil.

3. Place salmon on foil and evenly top with butter, lemon juice, salt, and pepper.

4. Bake for 20 minutes, or until salmon flakes with fork.

5. Serve with Golden Encrusted Brussels Sprouts.

6. Serve with lemon wedges.

Golden Encrusted Brussels Sprouts - - - - - - - - - - - - - - - - - -

I believe brussels sprouts have an unfair and unfavorable reputation. When cooked correctly, these mini cabbages are divine. Serve with Lemon Butter Baked Salmon or Fish Sticks with Tartar Sauce (p. 139). Serves 6.

3 cups brussels sprouts

1 Tbsp. olive oil

2 Tbsp. butter

4 cloves fresh garlic

½ tsp. salt

½ tsp. pepper

1. Remove wilted leaves and brown spots from brussels sprouts. Cut each brussels sprout in half.

2. In large skillet over medium heat, cook olive oil and butter until melted.

3. Add brussels sprouts, garlic, salt, and pepper. Cook until golden encrusted and tender, about 10 minutes.

Lemon Garlic Grilled Salmon

SERVES 4

Salmon is one of my favorite fish. It is lovely infused with lemon juice and olive oil and grilled to perfection.

4 salmon filets

½ cup fresh squeezed lemon juice

⅓ cup extra-virgin olive oil

4 cloves garlic, minced

2 tsp. lemon zest

2 tsp. dill weed

½ tsp. celery salt

½ tsp. salt

½ tsp. fresh ground pepper

Blistered Green Beans (see next page)

- -

1. Place salmon filets in a single layer in greased 9 × 13 baking dish.

2. In medium bowl, combine lemon juice, olive oil, garlic, lemon zest, dill weed, celery salt, salt, and pepper.

3. Pour lemon mixture over salmon filets and let marinate for 10–15 minutes.

4. Grill salmon over medium coals for 5 minutes on each side, or until salmon is no longer translucent and flakes with a fork.

5. Serve with Blistered Green Beans.

Blistered Green Beans ----------------------------------

Broccoli is America's favorite vegetable, but my personal favorite is sautéed French string beans. They are simple but sophisticated. This is our go-to side dish that accompanies Lemon Garlic Grilled Salmon beautifully. Serves 6.

2 Tbsp. butter

3 cups French string beans

3 cloves fresh garlic

½ tsp. sea salt

½ tsp. pepper

1. In skillet, melt butter on medium heat.

2. Add beans and garlic cloves and sprinkle with sea salt and pepper.

3. Cook until blistered, starting to brown.

Fish Sticks with Tartar Sauce

SERVES 6

Even if your kids don't like fish, they will love these homemade fish sticks with homemade tartar sauce. The fish is mild, lightly breaded, and pan seared to create a crispy outer layer. Dipped in a creamy sauce, this is a great catch.

1 cup panko bread crumbs

2 Tbsp. finely shredded parmesan cheese

2 tsp. dried parsley

½ tsp. garlic powder

½ tsp. onion powder

½ tsp. salt

¼ tsp. pepper

1 egg

1 Tbsp. water

2 lbs. filet of sole, rinsed and cut into 4-inch by 2-inch pieces

¼ cup canola oil

1 lemon, quartered

Simple Tartar Sauce (see next page)

Golden Encrusted Brussels Sprouts (p. 135)

1. In small bowl, combine bread crumbs, cheese, parsley, garlic and onion powders, salt, and pepper. Place in shallow dish.

2. In another small bowl, whisk egg and water.

3. Lightly coat each fish piece with egg wash, followed by bread crumbs.

4. Heat oil in skillet over medium-high heat.

5. Add fish and cook on one side until golden, about 3 minutes. Turn and repeat.

6. Remove fish and place on paper towel–lined plate.

7. Serve with lemon wedges, tartar sauce, and brussels sprouts.

Simple Tartar Sauce --

This recipe calls for two ingredients and can be whipped up in seconds. How easy is that?
Serves 8.

1 cup mayonnaise

¼ cup dill relish

1. In small bowl, combine ingredients.

Cooking Measurement Equivalents

Cups	Tablespoons	Fluid Ounces
⅛ cup	2 Tbsp.	1 fl. oz.
¼ cup	4 Tbsp.	2 fl. oz.
⅓ cup	5 Tbsp. + 1 tsp.	
½ cup	8 Tbsp.	4 fl. oz.
⅔ cup	10 Tbsp. + 2 tsp.	
¾ cup	12 Tbsp.	6 fl. oz.
1 cup	16 Tbsp.	8 fl. oz.

Cups	Fluid Ounces	Pints/Quarts/Gallons
1 cup	8 fl. oz.	½ pint
2 cups	16 fl. oz.	1 pint = ½ quart
3 cups	24 fl. oz.	1½ pints
4 cups	32 fl. oz.	2 pints = 1 quart
8 cups	64 fl. oz.	2 quarts = ½ gallon
16 cups	128 fl. oz.	4 quarts = 1 gallon

Other Helpful Equivalents

1 Tbsp.	3 tsp.
8 oz.	½ lb.
16 oz.	1 lb.

Metric Measurement Equivalents

Approximate Weight Equivalents

Ounces	Pounds	Grams
4 oz.	¼ lb.	113 g
5 oz.		142 g
6 oz.		170 g
8 oz.	½ lb.	227 g
9 oz.		255 g
12 oz.	¾ lb.	340 g
16 oz.	1 lb.	454 g

Approximate Volume Equivalents

Cups	US Fluid Ounces	Milliliters
⅛ cup	1 fl. oz.	30 ml
¼ cup	2 fl. oz.	59 ml
½ cup	4 fl. oz.	118 ml
¾ cup	6 fl. oz.	177 ml
1 cup	8 fl. oz.	237 ml

Other Helpful Equivalents

½ tsp.	2½ ml
1 tsp.	5 ml
1 Tbsp.	15 ml

Index

A

Alfredo and Fettuccine, Light: 91
Apple and Walnut Oatmeal: 22
Asparagus, Chicken, and Mushroom
       Fettuccine: 79

B

Bacon and Egg Omelet: 19
Bagel Breakfast Egg Sandwiches: 17
Bagels, Vegetable Cream Cheese and: 15
Bahama Chicken Soup: 56
Baked Salmon, Lemon Butter: 134
Bananas Foster French Toast: 20
Basil Butter Chicken: 93
Bean and Beef Burrito Supreme: 120
Bean Tostadas, Beef and: 127
Beef and Bean Tostadas: 127
Beef and Cheese Enchiladas: 116
Beef and Potato Soup, Hungarian: 58
Beef Burrito Supreme, Bean and: 120
Beef Stroganoff: 119
Beef Taco Salad, Green Chili and: 47
Berry Banana Morning Smoothie: 4
Biscuits and Gravy, Country: 18
Blistered Green Beans: 137
Blueberry Pancakes, Buttermilk: 12

Bolognese, Rigatoni: 80
Bow-Tie Carbonara: 78
Bread, Garlic: 87
Breakfast Sandwiches, Ham and Egg: 16
Brussels Sprouts, Golden Encrusted: 135
Burger Sliders, Garden: 111
Burrito Supreme, Bean and Beef: 120
Butter Chicken, Basil: 93
Buttermilk Blueberry Pancakes: 12

C

Caesar Chicken Salad: 41
Caesar Dressing, Creamy: 41
Caesar Tortellini Salad: 36
Caprese Sandwiches: 30
Carbonara, Bow-Tie: 78
Chalupas: 115
Cheese and Chicken Quesadillas: 106
Cheeseburger Soup: 63
Cheese Enchiladas, Beef and: 116
Cheese Ravioli with Creamy Marinara: 86
Cheese Roll-Ups, Ham and: 33
Cheesy Potato Soup: 51
Chicken, and Mushroom Fettuccine, Asparagus: 79
Chicken and Peanut Coleslaw Salad: 42
Chicken and Rice Casserole: 67

Chicken and Rice Soup: 59
Chicken and Stuffing Bake: 68
Chicken Divan: 69
Chicken Enchiladas: 76
Chicken Fajitas: 95
Chicken Noodle Casserole: 70
Chicken Noodle Soup, Chinese: 65
Chicken Noodle Soup, Classic: 52
Chicken Nuggets: 105
Chicken Parmesan: 104
Chicken Quesadillas, Cheese and: 106
Chicken Salad, Caesar: 41
Chicken Salad Croissants: 34
Chicken Soup, Bahama: 56
Chicken Spaghetti, Lemon: 81
Chicken Squares, Savory: 94
Chicken Taco Soup: 54
Chicken Taquitos: 96
Chili and Beef Taco Salad, Green: 47
Chili, Two-Bean: 60
Chinese Chicken Noodle Soup: 65
Classic Chicken Noodle Soup: 52
Club Wraps, Turkey: 27
Coleslaw Salad, Chicken and Peanut: 42
Corn Dogs: 124
Country Biscuits and Gravy: 18
Cream Cheese and Bagels, Vegetable: 15
Cream Sauce, Penne Pasta with Tomato: 88
Creamy Caesar Dressing: 41
Creamy Marinara, Cheese Ravioli with: 86
Croissants, Chicken Salad: 34
Cucumber Dill Tartar Sauce: 133

D

Dad's Pepper Steak: 112
Dill Poached Salmon, Lemon and: 132
Dill Tartar Sauce, Cucumber: 133
Divan, Chicken: 69
Dressing, Creamy Caesar: 41
Dressing, Ranch: 38
Dressing, Thousand Island: 29

E

Egg Breakfast Sandwiches, Ham and: 16
Egg Mini Frittatas, Sausage and: 10
Egg Omelet, Bacon and: 19
Egg Salad Sandwiches: 25
Eggs and Toast, Poached: 13
Egg Sandwiches, Bagel Breakfast: 17
Eggs Benedict: 8
Enchiladas, Beef and Cheese: 116
Enchiladas, Chicken: 76

F

Fajitas, Chicken: 95
Fettuccine, Asparagus, Chicken, and
        Mushroom: 79
Fettuccine, Light Alfredo and: 91
Fish Sticks with Tartar Sauce: 139
Fish Tacos: 130
French Toast, Bananas Foster: 20
Fresh Salsa: 107
Frittatas, Sausage and Egg Mini: 10

G

Garden Burger Sliders: 111
Garden Salad, Italian: 37
Garlic Bread: 87
Garlic Grilled Salmon, Lemon: 136
Garlic, Sautéed Spinach and: 133
Golden Encrusted Brussels Sprouts: 135
Gravy, Country Biscuits and: 18
Green Beans, Blistered: 137
Green Chili and Beef Taco Salad: 47
Green Onion and Lemon–Crusted Halibut: 129
Grilled Salmon, Lemon Garlic: 136

H

Halibut, Green Onion and Lemon–Crusted: 129
Ham and Cheese Roll-Ups: 33
Ham and Egg Breakfast Sandwiches: 16
Ham, Pan-Roasted Potatoes and: 7
Hawaiian Haystacks: 103
Hawaiian-Style Meatballs: 123
Hollandaise Sauce: 9
Honey Mustard: 33
Honey Mustard Chicken: 99
Hungarian Beef and Potato Soup: 58

I

Italian Garden Salad: 37

K

Kebabs, Prosciutto Salad: 38

L

Lemon and Dill Poached Salmon: 132
Lemon Butter Baked Salmon: 134
Lemon Chicken Spaghetti: 81
Lemon–Crusted Halibut, Green Onion and: 129
Lemon Garlic Grilled Salmon: 136
Light Alfredo and Fettuccine: 91

M

Macaroni and Cheese: 82
Manicotti Shells, Stuffed: 85
Marinara, Cheese Ravioli with Creamy: 86
Marinara Meatball Sandwiches: 32
Meatballs, Hawaiian-Style: 123
Meatballs Sandwiches, Marinara: 32
Mom's Tuna and Pasta Shell Salad: 48
Mushroom Fettuccine, Asparagus, Chicken, and: 79

N

Navajo Tacos: 113
Noodle Casserole, Chicken: 70

O

Oatmeal, Apple and Walnut: 22
Oatmeal, Peaches and Cream: 23
Omelet, Bacon and Egg: 19

P

Pancakes, Buttermilk Blueberry: 12
Pan-Roasted Potatoes and Ham: 7
Parmesan, Chicken: 104
Pasta Shell Salad, Mom's Tuna and: 48
Peaches and Cream Oatmeal: 23
Peanut Coleslaw Salad, Chicken and: 42
Penne Pasta with Tomato Cream Sauce: 88
Pepper Steak, Dad's: 112
Philly Cheesesteak Sandwiches: 28
Poached Eggs and Toast: 13
Poached Salmon, Lemon and Dill: 132
Pomodoro Sauce and Spaghetti: 84
Popcorn Chicken: 100
Potatoes and Ham, Pan-Roasted: 7
Potato Soup, Cheesy: 51
Potato Soup, Hungarian Beef and: 58
Prosciutto Salad Kebabs: 38

Q

Quesadillas, Cheese and Chicken: 106
Quick Taco Soup: 53

R

Ragù Sauce, Spaghetti with: 89
Ranch Dressing: 38

Ravioli with Creamy Marinara, Cheese: 86
Reuben Sandwiches: 29
Rice Casserole, Chicken and: 67
Rice Soup, Chicken and: 59
Rigatoni Bolognese: 80
Roll-Ups, Ham and Cheese: 33

S

Salad Kebabs, Prosciutto: 38
Salmon, Lemon and Dill Poached: 132
Salmon, Lemon Butter Baked: 134
Salmon, Lemon Garlic Grilled: 136
Salsa, Fresh: 107
Sauce and Spaghetti, Pomodoro: 84
Sauce, Cucumber Dill Tartar: 133
Sauce, Hollandaise: 9
Sauce, Penne Pasta with Tomato Cream: 88
Sauce, Simple Tartar: 140
Sauce, Spaghetti with Ragù: 89
Sauce, Special: 111
Sausage and Egg Mini Frittatas: 10
Sautéed Spinach and Garlic: 133
Savory Chicken Squares: 94
Seasoning Mix, Taco: 127
Shepherd's Pie: 72
Simple Tartar Sauce: 140
Sliders, Garden Burger: 111
Smoothie, Berry Banana Morning: 4
South-of-the-Border Soup: 62
Spaghetti, Lemon Chicken: 81
Spaghetti, Pomodoro Sauce and: 84
Spaghetti with Ragù Sauce: 89

Special Sauce: 111
Spinach and Garlic, Sautéed: 133
Steak, Dad's Pepper: 112
Stroganoff, Beef: 119
Stuffed Manicotti Shells: 85
Stuffing Bake, Chicken and: 68
Sweet and Sour Chicken: 98

T

Taco Salad: 45
Taco Salad, Green Chili and Beef: 47
Taco Salad, Walking: 44
Taco Seasoning Mix: 127
Tacos, Fish: 130
Tacos, Navajo: 113
Taco Soup, Chicken: 54
Taco Soup, Quick: 53
Tamale Pie: 74
Tamale Topping: 75
Taquitos, Chicken: 96
Tartar Sauce, Cucumber Dill: 133
Tartar Sauce, Fish Sticks with: 139
Tartar Sauce, Simple: 140

Tater Tot Casserole: 73
Tempura Vegetables: 109
Teriyaki Chicken: 108
Thousand Island Dressing: 29
Toast, Bananas Foster French: 20
Toast, Poached Eggs and: 13
Tomato Cream Sauce, Penne Pasta with: 88
Tortellini Salad: 39
Tortellini Salad, Caesar: 36
Tortilla Strips: 55
Tostadas, Beef and Bean: 127
Tuna and Pasta Shell Salad, Mom's: 48
Turkey Club Wraps: 27
Two-Bean Chili: 60

V

Vegetable Cream Cheese and Bagels: 15

W

Walking Taco Salad: 44
Walnut Oatmeal, Apple and: 22
Wraps, Turkey Club: 27

- 1ST PLACE
Dream Dinners Contest
- 2ND PLACE
BBQ Lover's Contest
- 3RD PLACE
Utah's Own Ultimate
Recipe Round-Up

Also By Shauna Evans

Whether you're looking for a savory barbecue sauce for your next backyard get-together or a showstopping dessert, you've come to the right kitchen to find it.

Discover top-secret family recipes like Evans Family Award-Winning Fudge and German Plum Streusel! You will never be at a loss for great-tasting meals when you have these easy award-winning recipes at your side!

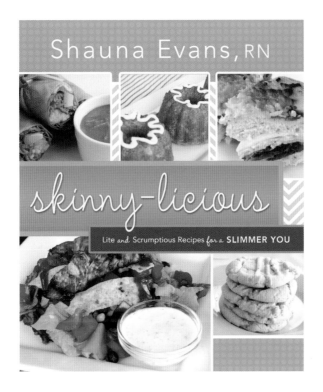

Also By Shauna Evans

E at yourself skinny! Registered nurse and award-winning cook Shauna Evans proves that you don't need to give up your favorite foods in order to slim down.

You can enjoy tasty recipes like Lime and Cilantro Shrimp Skewers, Stuffed Red Peppers, and Cherry Chocolate Cake, all while losing weight and feeling great. Healthy cooking has never been easier!

About the Author

Shauna Schmidt Evans was born and raised in northern Utah beneath the Wasatch Mountains. She was a competitive athlete. Her high school cheer squad was ninth in the nation, and she took fourth place in her age category when she ran her first St. George marathon at the age of eighteen. She has completed three half marathons and three full marathons.

Shauna graduated from Brigham Young University with a bachelor of science in nursing. At BYU, she taught in the anatomy lab. She married Joe Evans, BYU backup quarterback to Ty Detmer, in 1992. They have five fit, athletic children. Shauna is a water aerobics instructor and continues her nursing education in subjects regarding nutrition, exercise, and overall good health. Health and fitness have always been of special interest to her.

Shauna is the author of *What Goes with What for Baby Rooms: Decorating Made Easy*, *Sweet and Savory: Award-Winning Recipes Made Easy*, and *Skinny-licious: Lite and Scrumptious Recipes for a Slimmer You*. She has won over ten recipe contests; has appeared on *The Daily Dish*, *Good Things Utah*, *Studio 5*, and *Fox 13 News*; and has taught at the Salt Lake Home Show.